D0225536

Small Business and Society

Social analysis

A series in the Social Sciences
Edited by Richard Scase, University of Kent

Beyond Class Images: Explorations in the Structure of Social Consciousness
Howard H. Davies

Fundamental Concepts and the Sociological Enterprise
C. C. Harris

Urban Planning in a Capitalist Society
Gwyneth Kirk

The State in Western Europe
Edited by Richard Scase

Autonomy and Control at the Workplace: Contexts for Job Redesign
Edited by John E. Kelly and Chris W. Clegg

The Entrepreneurial Middle Class
Richard Scase and Robert Goffee

Capitalism, the State and Industrial Relations: The Case of Britain
Dominic Strinati

Alcohol, Youth and the State
Nicholas Dorn

The Evolution of Industrial Systems
Timothy Leggatt

Sociological Interpretations of Education
David Blackledge and Barry Hunt

Sociological Approaches to Health and Medicine
Myfanwy Morgan, Michael Calnan and Nick Manning

School Organisation: A Sociological Perspective
William Tyler

Entrepreneurship in Europe
Edited by Robert Goffee and Richard Scase

The Theory and Philosophy of Organizations: Critical Issues and New Perspectives
Edited by John Hassard and Denis Pym

Small Business and Society

David Goss

London and New York

UNIVERSITY
OF NEW BRUNSWICK

AUG 27 1992

LIBRARIES

First published 1991
by Routledge
11 New Fetter Lane, London EC4P 4EE

Simultaneously published in the USA and Canada
by Routledge
a division of Routledge, Chapman and Hall, Inc.
29 West 35th Street, New York, NY 10001

© 1991 David Goss

Typeset from Author's disks by J&L Composition Ltd.,
Filey, North Yorkshire

Printed and bound in Great Britain by
Mackays of Chatham PLC, Chatham, Kent

All rights reserved. No part of this book may be reprinted or
reproduced or utilized in any form or by any electronic,
mechanical, or other means, now known or hereafter invented,
including photocopying and recording, or in any information
storage or retrieval system, without permission in writing from
the publishers.

British Library Cataloguing in Publication Data
Goss, David, 1956–
    Small Business and Society – (Social Analysis)
    1. Great Britain. Small firms
    I. Title II. Series
    338.6420941

    ISBN 0–415–04989–X

Library of Congress Cataloging in Publication Data
Goss, David, 1956–
    Small Business and Society/David Goss.
    p. cm.–(Social analysis)
    Includes bibliographical references and index.
    ISBN 0–415–04989–X (HB)
    1. Small business–Social aspects–Great Britain. 2. Small
    business–Great Britain. I. Title. II. Series.
    HD2346.G7G67 1991
    306.3′4–dc20   90–37091
                                                         CIP

To Fiona, Sophie and Charlotte

Contents

Figures and tables

Preface

This book was written out of a long-standing interest in the sociology of small business that developed during my studies at the University of Kent. This interest was stimulated by my own experiences of working in small firms and by the feeling that a great deal of the material I was reading seemed to have very little in common with the ways in which I had found small firms to operate. Much of the literature seemed either overly simplistic, naively romantic, or thoroughly dogmatic. Thankfully things have improved since then, but I feel there is still a need for the critical, or at least sceptical, analysis of small business to be further developed. My concern, therefore, has been to go some way towards providing such an analysis and, at the same time, to bring together in a manner accessible to those without a specialist interest in this field, a range of research data and theoretical argument that has hitherto been limited to a more specialist readership. It is hoped that in this respect the book will be of some use to students undertaking both introductory and specialist courses in small business as well as to those more interested in the sociological arguments.

There are many people without whose help, interest and kindness this book would not have been possible. I owe a special debt to the late Derek Allcorn, whose encouragement, patience and friendship got me into academic research and who taught me much more than I realized at the time. Also to Dick Scase for his continued and much appreciated advice and support. Last, and by no means least, I have to thank my family, especially Fiona, Sophie and Charlotte, who have not only suffered my 'thinking' with unbelievable tolerance and good humour, but have also provided more support than I could rightly have asked for. My thanks to all.

Acknowledgements

The author would like to thank the following sources for their kind permission to reproduce material in this volume: Basil Blackwell for Table 7.1; the Controller of Her Majesty's Stationery Office for Tables 2.1, 2.5 and 7.2; the *International Small Business Journal* for the extract from J. Curran and J. Stanworth (1989) 'Education and training for enterprise', vol. 7.2; the *Journal of General Management* for Table 5.1; *Management Education and Development* for Figure 3.1n, which first appeared in vol. 20, 2; the Small Business Research Trust for Tables 2.3, 2.4, 2.6, 2.7, 3.1 and 2.1n; Unwin Hyman for Figure 3.1 and the extract from R. Goffee and R. Scase (1985) *Women in Charge*.

Introduction

Less than a decade ago, as small business nudged its way on to the political agenda, it could justifiably be claimed that this was an area about which social scientists knew relatively little but needed to know more. Today such a claim requires qualification. There is now no shortage of published research on virtually all aspects of small business, and for the interested reader there is available a mass of social scientific literature and research. Virtually all social scientific disciplines, from sociology and psychology to political science, economics and human geography, have contributed to this stock of knowledge, as have numerous practically oriented writers offering advice through small business start-up guides and regular small business features in newspapers and journals. Writing about small business is now very big business indeed.

Such plenitude, however, has brought its own difficulties. The problem for the student of small business is twofold. On the one hand, there is the sheer heterogeneity of the academic literature, both in terms of the variety of empirical content and the inconsistency of definition and methodology. On the other hand, the strong polemical overtones which have come to characterize debate in this field have made it difficult to disentangle political dogma and idealistic speculation from reasoned argument and objective research. It is hoped that the following pages will clarify these issues and make the understanding of small business and its position in contemporary society more accessible to those without a specialist interest in the field. As such this is a book which attempts to make sense of the argument and debate surrounding small business rather than to provide prescriptions about what small business ought to be or how small firms should be run.

The origins of the present boom in small-business research can be traced back to the Bolton Report, published in 1971. Whatever its faults, this report was successful in sowing in the minds of business commentators and academics the seeds of the notion that small business was, or more precisely had, a problem. The volume of research grew steadily though unspectacularly throughout the 1970s and ranged over such issues as the social class position of small shopkeepers, the economic decline of small firms, small business industrial relations, and, of course, the doctrine of 'small is beautiful'. The 1979 election of Margaret Thatcher's Conservative government, however, saw the steady stream of small business research turn into a torrent as political ideology thrust small business issues to the forefront of the struggle to revitalize the flagging fortunes of the British economy. Political topicality, it seems, is a kind parent to research funding; not only the volume of small business research but also its scope and breadth have expanded during the Thatcher years. Thus by 1987 it was possible for the London Business School's annual *Small Business Bibliography* to include such diverse headings as Entrepreneurship, Entrepreneurs in Economic and Social Development, The Entrepreneurial Personality, Female Entrepreneurs, Industrial Relations, Marketing, Education and Training, Technology and Innovation, Legislation, Bankruptcy, Co-operatives, Job Generation, Minorities in Small Business, Government Policy, and Socio-economic Environment.

If such diversity does not complicate the process of analysis sufficiently there are additional hazards to be negotiated in the form of the polemical and ideologically slanted interventions that have encroached upon this field of study. The most forceful of these has been launched from within the ranks of supporters of free-market capitalism. The emergence of right-wing governments in the UK and USA in particular has proved a fertile breeding ground for the idea that the health of small business is a key indicator of the economic and political health of a nation. Indeed, for sympathizers with this position small business takes on an almost messianic role, with an attendant leaning towards hyperbole and the almost wilful disregard of evidence that casts small firms in anything other than a favourable light. Most marked in this respect have been pronouncements relating to the job-generating potential of small business and its role in the regeneration of the spirit of enterprise and innovation which, all too frequently, have been made on the flimsiest of evidence and in terms which defy objective verification.

None the less, the vigour with which the right has promoted the virtues of small business has partially been matched by those on the political left, who have countered with suitably vitriolic critiques of the small firm across a range of issues. Generally these attacks have emphasized the negative aspects of small firms, such as their poor record in terms of employment conditions, autocratic employer control and poor safety standards. But they have also drawn attention to the economically dependent position of small business, arguing that the health of small firms is ultimately dependent upon the position of large capitalist enterprises: large capital will allow small business to thrive only so long as it is profitable for it to do so. In this respect the growth in small business activity of the 1980s represents a strategy on the part of large firms to divest certain of their less profitable activities to subcontracted small businesses which can operate with greater flexibility and at lower cost on account of their 'freedom' from trade unions and, hence, greater opportunity for the 'hyper-exploitation' of labour.

A third contender in the debate about small business has been the Green movement. Interest from this direction has been stimulated by disenchantment with the quality of life provided by advanced industrial societies and discontent at the environmental damage inflicted by large-scale industry. Small organization, therefore, represents a natural alternative to such methods, a view stimulated by the influential work of Fritz Schumacher, inventor of the slogan 'small is beautiful'. From within this camp, however, the picture of smallness which emerges often appears as a romanticized response to the perceived iniquities of 'bigness', a knee-jerk reaction frequently characterized by confusion and inconsistency, particularly in relation to issues such as ownership and control, technological development, and state regulation. Nevertheless, this is likely to be a dimension of the small business argument that will increase in significance if, as seems likely, Green politics continue their ascendency.

Chapter one examines the origins and theoretical bases of these three positions with the intention of clarifying the parameters within which contemporary small-business debate is being conducted. In an attempt to compensate for some of the inadequacies of these polemical positions, an alternative 'sociological' conception of small business is suggested, a conception which is more amenable to the empirical diversity and complexity which characterizes this area of economic activity.

Indeed, although there can be few aspects of small business remaining unexplored, the growth in research reports has done little to remove confusion or generate agreement. It seems almost that the more that is discovered about small business the more problems of interpretation arise. Chapter two, therefore, attempts to unravel some of the ambiguities of empirically based small business research and to provide a profile of the activity of small firms in the UK based upon the most recently available data. The most intractable problem in this area stems from the absence of any agreed definition of what actually constitutes a small firm and the lack of reliable and inclusive data-bases. But even when these difficulties have been taken into account the sheer diversity of small-business activity remains to be faced. Small firms are active in virtually all sectors of the economy, employing processes and technologies and generating services of the most varied kinds. Unfortunately, the obvious methodological difficulties which such a situation implies for analysis have frequently been overlooked in small business research. In particular, the use of universal conceptions of the small firm is commonplace, as is the assumption that it is meaningful to speak of a homogeneous 'small firm sector'. Utilizing the conceptual framework developed in Chapter one, it is suggested that the latter difficulties can be circumvented by an analysis rooted in substantive social relations rather than formal categories.

The principal thrust of the approach developed in these two chapters is to emphasize the diversity and complexity of small business activity and the ways in which this is affected by contextual and environmental factors. Little support is given to the notion that the social nature of small business is a function of some essential quality of smallness per se. This idea is amplified and extended throughout the following chapters, where attention is focused on specific issues concerning the position of small businesses in contemporary society.

The first to come under scrutiny is entrepreneurship and the social and psychological characteristics of small business owners. Very often, small business has been understood in terms of the distinctive psychological qualities of the entrepreneur, qualities that are usually framed in terms of individualism, achievement orientation and a general moral endorsement of capitalist market society. Whilst this may apply in some situations, Chapter three does show this conception to be unsatisfactory as a generalization. The case for the conclusive attribution of distinct entrepreneurial personality traits is less than convincing, as is the notion that all small business owners are fervent supporters of unrestrained market forces. In fact it seems that social factors such as socioeconomic class background, gender, ethnicity, and previous occupational experience are equally, if not more, useful than individual psychology in explaining the motives and actions of those who enter small business.

This conclusion is echoed in Chapter four where the emphasis shifts from those who own and run small businesses to those who are employed in them. Conventionally, employment relations within small firms have been thought of as essentially harmonious, and small business workers as possessing a deferential and non-economistic outlook. Such workers have been supposed to place great store by close personal relations with their employer and to exhibit higher levels of organizational attachment than their counterparts in large firms. The problem with this view, however, is that it derives in large part from the opinions of employers and from the intuitive observations of those sympathetic to small business interests. When the motives and definitions of workers themselves are held up to rigorous analysis, a very different picture emerges. It appears that a great deal of the acquiescent behaviour of workers in small firms derives not simply from subjective deference or loyalty to an employer, but from a pragmatic awareness of the limits of their power to challenge the latter's authority within the work situation. The nature of small business employment relations is thus a great deal more complex and contingent than the popular image would imply, an outcome of power and subjectivity rather than mere attitudinal affectation (Knights and Willmott 1989).

Chapter five continues the exposure of complexity by examining alternative forms of small business activity. Such forms can range from criminal entrepreneurship (such as dealing in stolen property or illegal substances, and prostitution), through trading in the black economy as a means of tax avoidance and/or supplementing welfare benefit, to micro-businesses operated part-time on the fringes of the formal economy, and unconventional forms of business organization. Of the latter, co-operatives and franchised small firms are the most notable. Both these forms of small business have increased rapidly throughout the 1980s, although they still represent a relatively small proportion of all small firms. Producer co-operatives have traditionally been associated with the political left and labour idealism or, at least, with an alternative approach to capitalistically organized work processes. Whilst many co-operatives are still motivated by such ideals, this form of organization appears also to have attracted those with more pragmatic objectives. Co-operatives have thus been encouraged as a means of creating jobs amongst the unemployed, on the grounds that this form of organization will prove more attractive than a conventional business to those disillusioned by job loss and recession. Although this may be so, such co-operatives have to face not only problems associated with likely deficiencies in skills and experience amongst members but also the absence of a unifying ideology or *raison d'être*.

Their long-term success is thus even more fragile than that of other co-operatives.

In marked contrast to co-operatives (of whatever sort), which are frequently isolated and insecure in the business world, franchised small businesses appear to have many advantages. These are formally independent enterprises that are simultaneously tied to a larger organization which provides them with an established product or service backed by a sales and supplies support network in exchange for a royalty on sales. Although a relatively secure form of business activity, some uncertainty remains as to whether franchised outlets are genuinely independent businesses or merely branches of a larger organization. On balance, a case can be made for viewing them as 'legitimate' small firms, albeit of a different type to conventional small businesses.

Such doubts do not arise in the case of high-technology small businesses, even though these often exhibit marked dissimilarities with other forms of small business. Nevertheless, new technology and innovation have frequently been regarded as the natural associates of small business, the latter providing a vehicle for the 'technological entrepreneur' or a convenient organizational form for realizing the potential of increasingly compact and decentralizing micro-electronic technologies. In both respects small firms have been cast by their supporters as vanguards for a process of industrial regeneration. Here, as in other areas, however, the available research severely qualifies any such straightforward conclusions. As Chapter six shows, not only are there serious reservations about what appears to be an unacceptable level of conceptual laxity (associated especially with terms like 'industrial regeneration' and 'reindustrialization'), but the specification of crucial notions such 'new technology' and 'high technology' is often left disturbingly vague. When this conceptual repertoire is tightened to an acceptable level the 'inevitable' link between small business and new technology is significantly weakened.

Such conceptual liberties, of course, are not restricted to the area of new technology. As Chapter seven reveals, they have also been taken, perhaps with more serious consequences, in the area of small-business policy. Since 1979 the volume of policy affecting small businesses, either directly or indirectly, has mushroomed. On the one hand, legislative changes have progressively removed categories of small firms from significant areas of statutory regulation, or lessened the 'burden' of regulation in areas such as financial control, health and safety, employment protection and taxation. On the other hand, indirect policy initiatives such as small business start-up schemes, enterprise agencies and small business training courses have multiplied. But in an area where considerable sums of money have been spent, efforts to monitor and evaluate the effectiveness of such policies have frequently been limited and less than conclusive. This has prompted some commentators to observe that small-business policy seems driven more by political expediency and the ideological quest to promote an 'enterprise culture' than by considerations of social benefit or value-for-money. Although there may be some truth in this, it is not the whole picture. Policy-makers, like researchers, can also fall victim to the extreme heterogeneity of small business activity, a heterogeneity that mitigates against both the development and assessment of policy initiatives on anything other than a relatively restricted scale.

It is hoped that the following chapters, taken together, provide a useful introduction to the social analysis of small business and the strengths and weaknesses of the arguments that have emerged in this increasingly debated area.

Chapter one

Theories of small business and society

To make sense of the debates and issues which surround small business it must be appreciated that this is an area where no one 'correct' explanation is to be found. Rather, there are a number of competing, and sometimes conflicting, perspectives and outlooks. These perspectives make different assumptions about the nature of society, of business in general and, as a result, of small business in particular.

The purpose of this chapter, therefore, is to show, as dispassionately as possible, the assumptions which underlie the key 'frames of reference' used to understand small business. It will consider the evidence and argument utilized in support of each case, and the lessons to be learned from them. Armed with this basic knowledge, readers will be better placed to judge for themselves how far theoretical assumptions have coloured the work of small business writers and what this means for the adequacy of their statements.

For this purpose it is convenient to distinguish between three theoretical 'frames of reference': the free-market model; the Marxian model; and the Green or ecological model. These can be regarded as representing extreme and opposing positions on the economic and political map of small-business polemic and, together, demonstrate clearly why this area has attracted its fair share of controversy and debate. Less directly polemical and of growing importance is an increasingly sophisticated sociological understanding of small business which, in the final section of this chapter, is shown to improve upon the other approaches.

Small business and free-market theory

Few could question the fact that in the UK more or less rigorous versions of free market ideology have dominated 'official' thinking about small business in the 1980s, and that the proselytizing zeal of

Margaret Thatcher's Conservative government has raised small business to a position of prominence unparalleled in the post war decades. Although historically a place for small business has always existed in free-market thinking, in the UK at least, this tended to be implicit and taken for granted: a subsidiary component rather than a central plank of theory. Throughout the 1980s, however, there has occurred a good deal of free-market 'revisionism' in this respect, requiring some detailed elaboration.

The theory of the free market envisages a society constituted through the act of exchanging goods, services and individual capacities in the market. In such a society the principal actors are individuals who have unrestricted access to, and power to dispose of, the key factors of production, land, labour and capital, and the goods and services produced thereby. The result is widespread competition between buyers and between sellers in line with supply and demand – the balance of which determines the prices at which commodities will exchange. Thus, depending upon consumer preferences and resources, some goods and services will sell better than others, with the result that the sellers of demanded goods will be able to cover their costs and perhaps make a profit, whilst those whose goods are not in demand will have to risk either not selling them or reducing the price and selling them at a loss.

Within this economic framework small business now plays a crucial role. To begin with, small-scale enterprises represent the bulk of the stock of competing suppliers who jostle to fulfil consumer demand and thus ensure productive efficiency and maximum utility. And, as a corollary, small business is the natural avenue through which individuals with the ability, energy and ambition can apply their skills in the market to the benefit of themselves and society in general.

Accordingly, the biggest economic danger envisaged within the free-market perspective is the emergence of monopoly. Monopolies distort the operation of the market and prevent its self-regulating price-setting and distributive mechanisms from operating optimally. Consumer choice is narrowed, prices are kept artificially high, and supply is determined, not by demand, but by the interests of the monopolist. Simultaneously, the dynamism of the market is subdued as monopolies use their dominance to prevent new suppliers entering the market, having already absorbed or driven out all other competition. Thus, an economy in which monopoly organizations (including trade unions as monopoly suppliers of labour) dominate is one in which small business cannot survive for long – to the detriment of society in general. The availability of free choice in the market is thus vital to the

9

health of small business which should be free to operate un-encumbered by restrictive practices intended to protect monopoly interests, whether of business cartels, government or trade unions.

Underlying these economic strands of free-market theory is, of course, a particular conception of human nature and individual psychology. The psychology of the free market rests, somewhat strangely it might seem, upon the assumption that the state of nature is one of benevolence and mutuality. Such benevolence and mutuality, however, are not purely altruistic but, rather, the product of a balanced appreciation of self-interest. As Samuel Smiles put it, the free market provides the opportunity for even the humblest members of society, if they are prepared to help themselves, to prosper and, by so doing, to serve the greater good: 'Riches and ease, it is perfectly clear, are not necessary for man's highest culture ... so far from poverty being a misfortune, it may by vigorous self help, be converted even into a blessing' (quoted in Anthony 1977:78).

Here, too, are the origins of the view that the human spirit responds best to insecurity, uncertainty and pressure of desperate circumstance. These conditions foster entrepreneurial action and stimulate market activity as individuals attempt, or are driven, to overcome them (Coyne and Binks 1983). There is, thus, an inherent resilience within the human spirit which, unconstrained by the state, will flourish in response to uncertainty and competition. This, according to Kirzner (1979), is the entrepreneurial element in human action.

For the best part of the twentieth century 'orthodox' economic theory has been out of sympathy with this free-market doctrine, favouring instead variants of Keynesian demand-management and increased state intervention in the market process (Stewart 1975). Keynesianism, however, was rejected by the Thatcher government which, backed by the economic and political philosophy of A. F. Hayek, has striven to revitalize the principles of the free market, placing a now explicit emphasis on the rejuvenation of small business. Whereas Keynesians advocated the quantification of macro-level economic factors to enable central control and planning, the 'new' Hayekians reassert the supremacy of the entrepreneur over the planner. The market from a Hayekian position is a 'process' sending signals about economic opportunities to those individuals alert enough to observe them and with the will to act on them. Free market economies are, by definition, entrepreneurial economies.

Assumptions such as these have underpinned much of the 1980s 'small business revivalism' that has elevated the small firm from a mere element of free-market theory to a celebrated and justificatory symbol for a far-reaching programme of economic, political and social change initiated by the Thatcher government under the banner of the Enterprise Culture (Burrows 1991).

For those sympathetic to this position, the under-developed nature of Britain's small-business economy, compared to those of major international competitors, is singled out as a key factor in any explanation of the industrial devastation caused by the recession of the late 1970s and early 1980s. The growth of collectivism in the economy (particularly nationalized industries, local authorities and trade unions) is held responsible for the overall decline in the competitiveness of industry, the preservation of inefficient industrial practices and, most crucially, the simultaneous weakening of small business. It follows that since small business is a vital component of a market economy, its diminished state will adversely affect the ability of such an economy to adapt and respond to change. Although not without a certain intuitive appeal, this proposition is difficult to verify empirically. Usually the best that can be said is that 'those industrial countries which [have] a coherent policy of supporting small firms, as an overt act of economic policy, [are] experiencing faster rates of growth than the UK economy' (J. Bolton, quoted in Rainnie 1989:15). The implication of this sort of argument is that small business in some way enhances economic performance, but this is to risk confusing causality with association. It could equally be argued that fast economic growth allows a supportive small-business policy to be developed, or that the association between the virility of small business and economic growth is contingent, both being dependent upon some other variable(s). In the absence of a standardized international small-business data-base, this type of argument is, alas, likely to remain more supposition than established fact.

In practice, of course, the Enterprise Culture's affection for small business is rooted as much in the latter's intangible qualities as in precise measures of its economic effectiveness. The first such intangible is the supposed contribution made by small business to freedom and democracy. As stated by Margaret Thatcher,

> Small businesses are the very embodiment of a free society – the mechanism by which the individual can turn his leadership and talents to the benefit of both himself and the nation. The freer the society, the more small businesses there will be. And the more small businesses there are, the freer and more enterprising that society is bound to be.
> (Quoted in Rainnie 1989: 19)

This, of course, is another area where proof of causality is virtually impossible. Even so, the available research evidence does suggest that this is a picture that has more to do with rhetoric than rigour. The notion that social mobility through entrepreneurship is primarily dependent upon individual 'personality traits', for example, receives little unqualified support from social scientific research (see Chapter three), and exceptions to the 'small business equals freedom' thesis are not difficult to find. Sweden, for instance, has relatively few small businesses but is, by almost any definition, a free society; conversely, Hong Kong suffers the opposite condition.

Another of the claimed 'benefits' is a connection between small-business ownership and a strong attachment to capitalist values. Thus, in addition to the sale of council houses and shares in former nationalized industries, the encouragement of individuals to start a small business or become self-employed has been hailed as another step on the road to the Enterprise Culture's goal of 'popular capitalism' – and another nail in the coffin of 'popular socialism'. In short, small business encourages an attitude of mind in which there is a positive association between entrepreneurship, individual success and the creation of wealth such that individuals view business start-up as a viable career alternative to conventional employment. There is, however, a growing body of research to suggest that the simple association of small business proprietorship with a conservative political orientation and/or adherence to 'core' capitalist values is, at best, an oversimplification and, at worst, something of a misrepresentation (see Chapter three for a full discussion of these factors). Such a view takes no account of elements such as occupational experience, socio-economic class, gender or ethnicity, all of which not only affect the beliefs and values of small-business owners, but also influence the level of success individuals experience in obtaining capital funding and support for their enterprise.

Equally importantly, it is suggested that as a consequence of their direct personal contact with their employer those employed in small firms can expect to experience a better 'quality' of employment relationship than is found in large enterprises. This, in turn, will lead not only to better industrial relations but also to due deference to the entrepreneurial ideal: small-firm workers can appreciate the risks taken by their employer and identify with the problems of running a successful business, thereby encouraging a more 'realistic' and responsible attitude. These matters will be explored in detail in Chapter four, but for present purposes it is sufficient to point out that such claims receive nothing like unequivocal support from available data. Indeed, the bulk of the evidence points not only to the existence of relatively poor terms and conditions for many small-firm workers, but also to the fact that, even for entrepreneurs themselves, a long-term 'career' in small business may carry considerable financial and personal risks. On this matter the enthusiastic proselytes of business start-up are relatively silent or suitably depreciative.

Indeed, from a critical perspective the Enterprise Culture's attachment to small business has been viewed not so much as an attempt to revitalize the health of the nation but rather as a component of 'a hidden agenda', concerned to undermine the power of trade unions and swing the balance of power in favour of employers: small firms have a lower level of union membership than large firms, there are fewer industrial disputes and the link between individual performance and job security is clear. As Scase and Goffee succinctly point out: 'in a nutshell [the government's] small business strategy offers a solution to one of the major problems confronting industry as diagnosed by employers, managers and politicians: that is the management of labour' (Scase and Goffee 1980:16).[1] Although the active operation of such a hidden agenda must remain a matter for speculation, the limitation of trade union powers and the individualization of employment relationships do figure prominently in Enterprise Culture philosophy and are highly congruent with the non-collectivist nature of small business.

So, current fashions notwithstanding, there are a number of problems associated with the free market championing of 'small business revivalism', problems which its own arguments do not easily dispel. This, however, is not the place for a full critique (see Burrows 1990); for present purposes it is sufficient simply to point to general difficulties relevant to small business.

The first is a problem of theory and practice, namely the apparent contradiction between the key tenet of free-market theory restricting the economic role of the state to that of minimum intervention, and the enthusiasm of the Thatcher government for state policies to assist small business (see Chapter seven below; Rainnie 1989:13). This paradox cannot be resolved adequately within the free market theory itself, except by recourse to the speculative assertion that once the 'spirit of enterprise' has taken root further assistance will no longer be required. Even so, the worry for free-market purists is that if small business does not live up to the high economic hopes its proponents have forecast, its political and ideological importance to government may be justification enough for continued state support.

13

A second difficulty of a more epistemic nature is that the free-market tradition encourages a bias in favour of small business – in other words, because of the premises of the theory, small business is afforded automatically a position which casts it in a distinctly 'favourable' light. This centrality is essentially an artefact of theory; it is not demonstrated empirically but, rather, taken as given. The result is a marked tendency to approach small business with a selective vision – attending to that which supports the theory but ignoring or marginalizing that which does not. The result, all too often, is an emotive and romanticized view of small business and exaggerated claims about its potential for social and economic regeneration (for examples see Storey and Johnson 1986). Largely as a result of this contrived preference there remain significant gaps in the free-market portrayal of small business; gaps which are 'explained away' rather than explained. There is, for instance, very little attention given to matters such as the level and consequences of failed entrepreneurship, to the poor wages and conditions faced by many workers in small firms, to the 'accident-proneness' of workers in small firms or to the high levels of unfair dismissals (Rainnie 1989; Pearson 1985; also Chapters four and seven of this book). These are matters which will be commented on in due course.

Small business and Marxian analysis

In the Marxist tradition small business has received a somewhat contradictory treatment. Until the 1980s it was regarded by 'orthodox' theorists as of minimal importance in advanced capitalist societies, a moribund relic of the nineteenth century. More recently, however, Marxist writers have been forced to address more adequately the stubborn persistence of small business and its increasing appearance in social policy and political discourse.

The orthodox view rests upon the doctrine of the 'increasing centralization and concentration of capital'. According to this stricture, there is an inevitable historical tendency within capitalism which brings about a progressive reduction in the number of capital units (enterprises) and, simultaneously, an increase in their size. In other words, market competition and the progressive development of large-scale technology produces giant enterprises that either drive small businesses out of existence or absorb them (Braverman 1974). The result, monopoly capitalism, is an economy dominated by a small number of very large firms. Small business becomes an increasingly untenable occupation and waged work for big business the only alternative. Thus society is polarized into two opposing classes: a small but increasingly powerful bourgeoisie and an increasingly impoverished and exploited proletariat.

For many Marxists this was not an unattractive notion, for it promised to bring together members of the working class in ever larger numbers and under ever more intolerable circumstances, thereby creating the conditions for revolutionary ferment. Not only this, the concentration of production in a few centralized units would mean that, following the proletarian revolution, it would be an easy matter for the victorious workers to seize the commanding heights of the economy and employ this productive capacity in the service of a socialist society. Such centralized control would be impossible if production remained scattered in the hands of isolated individuals. Belief in this doctrine partly explains why orthodox Marxism has a history of hostility towards small business, regarding it as a barrier to the full socialization of the means of production.

To accept the doctrine of centralization and concentration makes small business an irrelevance – it becomes exactly what free-market theory claims it is not, a decaying irrelevance, destined to disappear with the increase in monopoly power generally.

The limitations of this theoretically informed view, however, are readily apparent. Although the concentration of capital has taken place in all industrial capitalist societies, it has not done so to the same extent in all industrial sectors (Davis and Scase 1985). Similarly, whilst the absolute number of small firms has declined throughout the twentieth century they are still far from extinct and, in many cases, show no signs of becoming so: in several industrial sectors small firms have remained the dominant and typical form of business organization. Also, in many economies concentration of ownership has taken place without being reflected in the centralization of organization – a large economic enterprise may be composed of a number of relatively small and quasi-autonomous establishments.

Accounting for the stubborn persistence of small business has spurred some writers to disarm the evolutionary inevitability of the doctrine of concentration and centralization by emphasizing the inherent unevenness of this process. This allows the possibility that not all sectors of an economy will develop at the same pace or in exactly the same direction. It is therefore possible for modern monopoly sectors to exist alongside 'older' competitive (or non-monopoly) small-business sectors. (Even here, it should be noted, small business is still treated as something of an anachronism, albeit one which can now theoretically be tolerated.) All that now remains is to explain the nature of the relationship between monopoly and non-monopoly enterprises.

Most frequently enlisted to this service is the notion of the 'dual economy'. The persistence of small business is here attributed to a functional relationship with large monopoly enterprises. The basis for this relationship is a structural division between sectors of the economy: small business forms what is referred to as a 'secondary' or 'peripheral' sector (either within the economy at large or within a single industry); monopoly enterprises constitute the 'core' or 'central' sector. The secondary sector survives by dint of the fact that it provides goods and services cheaply and flexibly for core enterprises. By establishing subcontracting relationships with small businesses (for the supply of components, for example) big business provides itself with an economic 'cushion' against market instabilities. First, the subcontracting relationship can be terminated quickly and easily if market conditions demand, with the additional bonus that problems of spare capacity or laying off workers remain firmly with the small contractor. Second, the power which comes with market dominance can be used to wring concessions (e.g., over prices or delivery times) from small firms competing for vital contracts (Friedman 1977:24). From this standpoint small business is functionally necessary for the continued and stable profitability of large enterprises. Even in a climate of corporate expansion, large firms resist taking over all small firms because the latter, as independent units, afford a valuable degree of flexibility to larger enterprises. Indeed, it has been suggested that the recession of the 1980s has led large firms to experiment further in this direction, adopting strategies of fragmentation and decentralization in attempts to off-load the responsibilities for risk-taking and employment on to small firms (Schutt and Whittington 1984:17).

Thus, the condition of existence for small business is its continued functionality for big business. This, in turn, affects the nature of employment conditions within the small firm which must establish working patterns congruent with maximum flexibility of operation and competitiveness of service. To meet this need there develops within the labour market a division paralleling that between the core and peripheral economies. Core enterprises demand workers with particular skills, training and social characteristics, the latter generally based on culturally stereotyped perceptions of reliability, intelligence, adaptability and trustworthiness, the possession of which is usually associated with age, gender and ethnic identities (Reich 1973). Secondary enterprises, because of the unstable and poorly rewarded nature of their work, are either unable to attract such 'core employees' or regard them as unsuitable for their needs, preferring those without formal training (who command lower wages) and with relatively little bargaining power (who can be laid off and autocratically controlled with little fear of resistance). This, it is suggested, leads to a disproportionate representation of women, unskilled and young workers in small firms, and to relatively low wages and poor working conditions (Rainnie 1985:155). Once these employment patterns are entered into they become self-reinforcing to the extent that secondary-sector workers find it increasingly difficult to gain access to primary jobs as they lack the training and qualifications demanded by core employers and are perceived to possess undesirable work habits and unstable employment patterns. Thus, employment in small firms is not only likely to be unpleasant, it also effectively rules out other, more attractive, employment opportunities.

Associated with labour market status are different modes of managerial control within the workplace. Put crudely, core employers adopt strategies of 'relative autonomy', whereas secondary employers make use of 'direct control'. Under the latter regime the employer/manager exercises control directly and explicitly by means of the specification of work methods, close supervision, and veiled or open coercion (e.g., threat of dismissal). Relative autonomy, conversely, attempts to harness the adaptability of labour by giving workers the encouragement and opportunity to adapt to changing situations in a manner beneficial to the firm (Friedman 1977).

In summary, strategies of employer control correspond to the essential characteristics of core and secondary enterprises: the latter are generally small, technologically backward and ruled in an autocratic manner by owner-managers or their personal delegates; the former are large monopolistic enterprises characterized by well-defined managerial hierarchies, professional management and internal labour markets.

As yet there has been no need to consider the role of those who run small businesses other than as the 'automatic' instigators of economically determined strategies. This is not so much an oversight as a reflection of Marxism's concern with positions rather than people. The dominant concern of this tradition has been to analyse the ways in which the structure of society (itself determined by the nature of the economic base) patterns the social categories within which individuals conduct their lives (e.g., as members of the working class or the ruling class) and the nature of the relationships between the categories (in the example just used, one of exploitation of the former by the latter). As such, the actions of individuals are shaped not by independent consciousness or individual personality, but by the constraints of social structure and class membership.

Thus, it is the nature of the class to which small business owners belong – usually termed the petty bourgeoisie – that has preoccupied Marxist analysis (Wright 1978,1985; Poulantzas 1975; Scase 1982; Curran 1986). However, whilst agreeing that the petty bourgeoisie is 'located' between the two major classes of capitalist society[2] (the proletariat and the bourgeoisie) there has been less agreement over its precise boundaries. Poulantzas (1975:285), for example, envisages a class defined by the ownership of small scale productive property but an absence of waged labour – artisan producers where the same agent is both owner and possessor of the means of production, as well as direct producer. Wright (1978), on the other hand, considers this too narrow a definition and suggests that in addition to a class of small business owners defined according to Poulantzas's criteria there is also a 'contradictory class location' to which belong those proprietors who employ small numbers of wage workers but do not live solely by the exploitation of their labour (the latter being the qualification for membership of the bourgeoisie proper). This interstitial group (between the petty bourgeoisie and the bourgeoisie) he calls 'small employers'. As will be seen in the final section of this chapter, the usefulness of this distinction as a tool of small business analysis has been exploited outside the Marxist framework, primarily because Wright's interest is not with small business per se, but with the specification of class boundaries, the prediction of class alliances and the prospects for the class struggle in advanced capitalist societies.

Despite differences in emphasis there is a marked similarity between the free-market and Marxist approaches in the way in which small business is introduced into the general problematic. In both cases it appears in a role which has been written, in advance, to support theoretical presuppositions, rather than as an object of study in its own right. The result in both cases is a 'closed' and formal mode of analysis which elevates to the status of certainty many aspects of small business which are, in fact, contingent, and invokes a convenient myopia when faced with data which does not 'fit' its a prioristic strictures.

Within the Marxist tradition the result is a treatment of small business that is a 'mirror image' of that offered by free-market theory. Small firms are allocated a subsidiary role, either as an irrelevant remnant of an outmoded state of capitalist development or a residual sector dependent for its existence on its continued usefulness to big business.

As a consequence, the usefulness of the framework is limited by its simplistic and overgeneralized treatment of the negative aspects of the small firm and its environment. Similarly misleading is the supposedly clear-cut and strictly functional division between small, dependent 'secondary' enterprises and large, monopolistic 'core' firms – a division which, in practice, is likely to characterize only a small number of enterprises in relation to the total stock of small firms, and these primarily in the manufacturing sector (Hodson and Kaufman 1982; Chapter two of this book). Thus, little attention is given to those small businesses where relations of dependence with monopoly enterprises are of minor or variable importance (e.g., in the professions, small jobbing firms dealing directly with the public, and small businesses with a wide spread of customers from large firms or who provide a highly specialized, non-competitive service). Some attempt to remedy these deficiencies has been made by Rainnie (1989) who, whilst emphasizing that small business must be located within the general structural framework of capitalist relations of production, also points to the diversity of large–small business relations. Drawing on the theory of 'combined and uneven development' and the empirical work of Schutt and Whittington (1984), Rainnie offers a four-fold classification of small firms:

1 *Dependent small firms* These complement and service the activities of larger firms (e.g., through subcontracting). Their viability depends on the level of activity and the 'make or buy' decisions of these large 'patrons'. Such a situation places effective control in the hands of the large enterprise, a control which extends not only over financial matters but also over the organization of the labour process, e.g., by forcing the minimization of wage costs and the implementation of flexible working.
2 *Competitive independent small firms* These compete with large firms by intense exploitation of labour and of (often anti-quated) equipment. Even here, however, the rules of existence are laid down, if possibly unwittingly and unintentionally, by the large firm. In terms of industrial relations the result is, more often than not, hyper-exploitation of labour.
3 *Old independent small firms* These operate in niches of demand unlikely ever to be touched by large capital. This will often entail a hand-to-mouth existence, scraping around for a living. It is amongst this and the latter type of small business that sweat-shops are most likely to be found.

4   *New independent small firms*   Small firms operating in (often founding and developing) specialized markets, but remaining open to the potentially fatal attentions of large firms. In other words, small firms which, within a very wide reading of the term, conduct the product and market research which large firms then step in and develop (see Chapter six below).
(Rainnie 1989:85ff)

   Still the emphasis remains upon dependence and exploitation, however, and contributes to the Marxist tendency to overstate the inevitability of small firms as providers of 'secondary' employment conditions. There is no necessary reason why secondary economic status (i.e., being dependent upon large firms for business) should lead to secondary employment conditions (or vice versa). For example, some small firms, particularly in craft or high tech areas, may depend upon specialist workers whom they have to treat as 'central', regardless of the enterprise's economic relation with large firms. To depict small business employment conditions as characterized solely by poor wages and working conditions and autocratic control may not only hide a great deal of empirical variation but also obscure the possibility of workers gaining psychological satisfactions from aspects of employment in small-scale enterprises (Ingham 1970).
   A similar charge of one-dimensionality can be made against the tendency to analyse the class position of small-business owners rather than the actions through which they produce and reproduce their enterprises. Such an 'anti-humanist' structural formulation leads to a caricature of the small business proprietor as a reactionary and unprogressive force within capitalism (Marx and Engels 1975:64) and a ruthless exploiter of labour. There remains, then, a hiatus, a need for more attention to be paid to the empirical processes through which small business owners construct and give meaning to their actions, to understand how 'proprietorship is "carved" out of a process of capital accumulation' (Scase 1982:161). Thus, whilst the Marxist perspective offers a healthy counter to the idealized optimism of free-market theory, it too suffers from deficiencies, induced by reliance upon a deterministic theoretical framework with resulting over-simplification and a failure to connect with the complex and 'messy' reality of small business in advanced capitalist societies.

Small business: the Green approach

This label applies less to a single body of thought and more to a collection of ideas which have come to see small business as a means to the solution of a moral and environmental crisis within advanced industrial societies. Numbered among the key assumptions of this approach is the proposition that industrialization (in both the communist and capitalist world) has created a state of mind indifferent, even hostile, to any goal other than short-term material gain. This amoral materialism has sustained the indiscriminate use of large-scale production techniques to violate both finite natural resources and the freedom, creativity and spontaneity of individuals and societies. Small-scale enterprise, it is believed, is the natural antithesis to such developments. It possesses an essential quality which, in itself, is humane, non-violent and benign, captured in the slogan 'small is beautiful'.

The origins of this view are not easy to trace, although it seems to have found an early expression of sorts in the work of G. D. H. Cole and the guild socialists where, in the decades around the turn of the century, attention was focused on the antinomy between the alienating consequences of industrial production and the need for democratic control of the workplace.

Guild socialism, as expounded by Cole, provided an opposition to the deterministic character of Marxism and to the collectivism and statism of Fabian socialism, both of which placed the state, in one form or another, in a position of social primacy. Guild socialism favoured, amongst other things, the decentralization of social institutions and their subjection to popular democratic control. For this popular democracy to be effective, scale was an important issue:

> Make a man a voter among voters in a democratic community; it is at least a half-truth that the measure of control he will have will vary inversely to the total number of votes. So, in the workshop, the control of the individual will be real in most cases only if the workshop is small, unless, as in a coal mine, only the simplest and most uniform questions have, as a rule, to be decided.
>
> (quoted in Tomlinson 1982:58)

Thus, for the productive unit smallness appeared a precondition for effective industrial democracy. These ideas, however, were out of sympathy with the tide of the times. Mass production, collectivism, bureaucratization and centralization were the touchstones in politics, economics and culture, and in the years following the First World War the guild socialist notions of smallness, decentralization and individual accountability held little appeal, even for those on the political left.

By the 1920s guild socialism as a coherent political movement had effectively disappeared, and it was not until the 1950s that some of its central ideas, particularly those relating to the liberating effect of small-scale organization and decentralized government, were reformulated by the guru of 'non-violent' economics, Fritz Schumacher (who coined the phrase 'small is beautiful'). These ideas have since gained in influence and popularity within the ecological and environmental movements of developed and developing societies (McRobbie 1982).

Schumacher's socialism, if that it can be called, is based firmly in the realm of culture and ideas (a similar concern amongst the guild socialists led more orthodox socialists to brand them 'romantics'). Culture concerns the 'quality of life', whereas the realm of economics involves only the 'standard of living'. And for Schumacher, whilst a given standard of living could be achieved by capitalist economics, an acceptable quality of life was, ultimately, only obtainable through the rejection of capitalism. The purpose of socialism, therefore, should be 'to evolve a more democratic and dignified system of industrial administration, a more humane employment of technology, and a more intelligent utilisation of the fruits of human ingenuity and effort' (Schumacher 1974:218). And, according to Schumacher, the prospects for realizing such an idea lie in the question of scale, not only as it relates to the size of an enterprise, but also to patterns of ownership and control. Drawing heavily on Tawney (himself a contemporary 'supporter' of guild socialism), Schumacher makes the following distinction:

> As regards private property, the first and most basic distinction is between (a) property that is an aid to creative work and (b) property that is an alternative to it. There is something natural and healthy about the former; and there is something unnatural and unhealthy about the latter – the private property of the passive owner who lives parasitically on the work of others. (Schumacher 1974:220)

Thus, what is unpalatable for Schumacher is not private property as such, but rather its scale – it is beneficial so long as it is not divorced from work, and, clearly, such a divorce can only be protected against by small-scale organization. In summary, then, Schumacher's project rests upon the assumption that in small-scale enterprise, private ownership is 'natural, fruitful and just', but that these qualities disappear as size increases to the extent that 'in large scale enterprise, private ownership is a fiction for the purpose of enabling functionless owners to live parasitically on the labour of others'. Not only is this unjust, it also introduces an

irrational element that distorts all relationships within the enterprise (Schumacher 1974:223).

Within this perspective the case for small business is inescapable.
What is less clear, however, is the form that the 'business' component should take, and the nature of the relationship between
small businesses and larger economic or political organizations.
Schumacher seems to favour a form of co-operative ownership and
control (ultimately enforceable by the state), but this raises the
question of the inevitable hostility which 'shared ownership' would
arouse amongst those for whom small business represents an
avenue of personal mobility and independence, or who prize the
'right' of ownership above other benefits. It could, of course, be
suggested that such 'antisocial individualism' would be overcome
by long-term socialization and education, but such a prospect
(even if it were attainable) immediately isolates this approach
from small business as it is known to exist at present. (A cynic
might suggest that this is why a good deal of the work of
Schumacher's followers has been concentrated in developing
countries rather than the less receptive 'advanced' nations.) Even
if the co-operative ownership and control criterion is disregarded
in favour of a 'community' of small, independent producers it is
difficult to envisage how this could operate on anything other than
the terms of the wider capitalist market (without massive state
regulation and control) – in which case nothing has changed, and
the 'terrifying simplification' of quality to quantity remains intact.

Clearly, this view of small business and its role in the construction of an alternative social order is not derived from conventional
scientific or quasi-scientific presumptions and evidence but is
founded upon an undisguised moral essentialism (in Schumacher's
case, Buddhist) which takes as its starting point the assumption
that small *is* beautiful. Not surprisingly, therefore, interest is
focused on what small business could become rather than with
what it now is. This is, perhaps, the principal weakness; the
argument 'draws on emotions and the appeal of a new lifestyle
rather than any empirically derived information' (Cross 1983:86).
In this respect many of the basic assumptions are seriously open to
question, in particular those which see an inevitable association
between smallness and a natural and healthy environment. The view
that, for example, 'even autocratic control is no serious problem in
small-scale enterprise which, led by a working proprietor, has
almost a family character' (Schumacher 1974:221) appears naively
romantic when assessed in the light of historical and contemporary
evidence about small sweat-shops, particularly those dependent
upon unpaid family labour (Hoel 1982; Pearson 1985).

So, although this approach offers yet another facet of the potential within small business it, too, remains limited by the narrow assumptions upon which it is founded. Like the free-market and Marxist traditions, it is concerned more with prescribing what small business ought to be than with analysing what it actually is. It is with this point in mind that recent developments in the sociology of small business can be introduced.

The sociology of small business

One of the first major sociological contributions to the understanding of small business in the UK was made by Bechhofer *et al.* (1974) through their research on small shopkeepers. Their concern was to explore the social, political and economic situations of those employing (relatively) small amounts of capital in order to win their livelihood. Dependence upon petty property as a source of income could, they claimed, lead to a distinctive social outlook or world view:

> If we attempt to generalise about the economic orientations of our sample, it is this 'individualism' that emerges as the dominant theme. Shopkeepers prize 'independence': they feel that if a man is his own master, then success or failure depend directly upon his own efforts and energies [sic]. In an ideal world, hard work will bring its own rewards. Such a view leads to a distaste for those things which in any way threaten this lusty individualism and so we find when we look at answers to questions about political matters, that large bureaucratic organisations are mistrusted, trade unions heartily disliked and state intervention in the name of any form of planning regarded with great scepticism.
> (Bechhofer *et al.* 1974:478)

On the face of it this seems to confirm the free-market view of entrepreneurial psychology, but Bechhofer is neither unrealistic nor romantic about the consequences of 'independence' for many small-business owners. Often, he notes, it takes the form of long working hours in physically poor conditions amounting to an extreme form of 'self-exploitation'. Interestingly, a recent study (Aldrich *et al.* 1986:351) replicating aspects of the Bechhofer investigations produced not dissimilar results. In particular it confirmed that small shopkeepers are consistent Conservatives (although not necessarily enthusiastic ones), that they are recruited from a range of social backgrounds (especially from lower non-manual, and skilled manual strata), and that they are strongly individualistic politically, being against big government and trade unions.

Although the level of corroboration between the Bechhofer and Aldrich studies is high, it must be remembered that they deal with a very specific group of small businesses. Thus although the results may hold true for small shopkeepers, and despite Bechhofer's claim that this group is representative of 'a somewhat broader category of independent businesses', research from other areas suggests the need for caution in attempting such generalizations. In fact, as sociological research on small business has increased in quantity and sophistication, there has emerged a picture of complexity and diversity covering not only the motives of small-business owners, but also the conditions under which they, and those they employ, work.

Scase and Goffee (1981), for example, have found evidence of 'proletarian tendencies' and 'radical ... quasi-socialist attitudes' among self-employed craft-workers. Similarly, Curran (1987) has suggested that those who run small co-operatives do not necessarily exhibit the expected antipathy towards all government assistance, and may be enthusiastic about the support given by government-sponsored development agencies and local authorities. Newby's (1977) study of farm workers unearths the complexities of agrarian paternalism, showing this to be a means by which farmers 'legitimate' the starkly inegalitarian nature of the employment relationship rather than an example of deeply felt social harmony. Stanworth and Curran (1979:337) point out that employment relations in small firms are not 'magically rid of the contradictions of interest and outlook which inevitably surround economic activities in our society'; like those in larger organizations they are as much shaped by 'external' influences (such as industrial sub-cultures and labour market conditions) as by enterprise size per se. Finally, a study by the author (Goss 1986) of small businesses in the general printing industry shows employer attitudes towards trade unions to be far from unequivocal, some regarding collective bargaining, and even the closed shop, as convenient and beneficial institutions.

Such studies all have one thing in common: they take as their principal focus the social relationships at the heart of small-business organization. In other words, and in marked contrast to the other approaches, these sociological perspectives make the small firm the starting point for investigation and not a mere derivative of theory. This, of course, explains the greater tolerance of diversity; there is no need to reduce the reality of the small-business situation to some underlying and theoretically privileged

25

principal. Nevertheless, if this diversity is to be analysed rather than merely described, some conceptual framework is necessary.

In effect, it is necessary to move between two theoretical poles: the sociology of action and the sociology of structure. The former allows the comprehension of the meanings, motives and actions of those individuals who make up particular small businesses. Stanworth and Curran provide one such perspective, developed to understand the growth of small firms.

> [The] *social action* view of the small firm concentrates heavily on understanding the internal social logic of the small firm as a social grouping ... the key to growth lies in the meanings attached to participation in the firm by the actors involved ... definitions and meanings attached to situations are *socially generated*, *socially sustained* and ... *socially changed*. In other words, the social action perspective here links the meanings and actions of the small firm's participants with their wider social environment.
>
> (Stanworth and Curran 1982:157, emphasis in original)

Business growth, to continue Stanworth and Curran's case, is neither a matter of evolutionary progress nor an automatic adjunct of economic success. On the contrary, they suggest, the growth potential of a business will be determined largely by the *meaning* the entrepreneur attaches to growth; and, for many, other objectives may be defined as more important (e.g., job satisfaction or personal control). In other words, these meanings are not fixed and immutable but are being constantly negotiated and renegotiated through the experience of social interaction.

But what of the 'situations' and 'wider social environment' that were mentioned? What do these include, and what are their links with meanings, definitions and social interactions generated at the individual level? Here the social action perspective is less forthcoming and recourse must be made to structural concepts.

The sociology of structure draws attention to those aspects of society which exist externally to and independently of the individual and act as constraints upon his or her actions. These are factors which bear directly and indirectly upon the organization of work. The latter can include generalized cultural norms which assert, for example, the legitimacy of managerial authority and the employer's property rights in the enterprise. The former, more concretely, commonly include, the state of the local labour market, technology and its impact upon labour requirements and capitalization, demand for products or services and legal restraints upon employment or production. These will be reflected to a greater or lesser degree in the structure of the enterprise itself; that is the ways in which work is organized, the rules which govern it, and the authority which can be invoked in the process (Salaman 1986:26).

One of the more promising attempts to use these ideas in small business analysis has been made by Scase and Goffee (1980; 1982). These writers distinguish between four 'types' of small business on the basis of the relative mix of capital utilized and labour (of either the proprietor, workers, or both) employed. They suggest that different 'mixes' of labour and capital are associated with particular types of proprietorial *role* within the business. These different roles form the basis for their four-fold typology, thus:

> First, there are the *self employed* who work for themselves and formally employ no labour. However, they are often dependent on the unpaid services of others, particularly other family members . . . . Secondly, there are *small employers* who not only work alongside their employees but also undertake the administrative and managerial tasks associated with running their businesses. Thirdly, there are the *owner-controllers* who do not work alongside their employees but, instead, are solely and singularly responsible for the administration and management of their enterprises. Finally, there are *owner-directors* who own and control companies with management hierarchies and within which executive decision-making is delegated to senior management staff.
>
> (Goffee and Scase 1985:33; emphasis in original)

Here the structure of a small business not only impacts on the relationships between the participants but also reflects a range of determinants deriving from both the individual actors and the business environment. In an industry such as construction, for example, where the main requirement to start a business is technical skill rather than capital, the self-employed form is likely to predominate. In manufacturing, however, where both capital and the labour of others is generally necessary for a successful business, this form will be relatively rare. Similarly, in industries such as printing where labour is extensively unionized some proprietors may remain as small employers to limit the potential for union intervention in 'their' businesses which would occur if they were to expand their workforces and relinquish personal control. Those who possess what Stanworth and Curran (1982) describe as an 'artisan' identity (which prizes intrinsic job satisfaction, autonomy and 'being able to pick the persons you work with') are unlikely either to be satisfied or successful in owner-controller or owner-director type businesses. On the other hand, those who hold a 'managerial', identity (managerial excellence, business efficiency and performance are the valued goals) are unlikely to realize their ambitions as self-employed or small employers. In this respect there is likely to be some degree of 'fit' between the meanings, definitions and abilities of proprietors and workers, the structure of the business, and its environmental constraints.

From this rather schematic overview it can be suggested that the task of an adequate analysis of small business is to determine empirically and theoretically the nature of these inter-relationships and their role in affecting the organization of particular small businesses and the outcomes available to the actors concerned. On this basis the three polemical approaches considered earlier are clearly inadequate in that their reliance upon prior theoretical imperatives encourages the real diversity and complexity of small business to be explained away rather than explained. In short, they provide an understanding that is simultaneously ideologically slanted and oversimplified. The issue of oversimplification in small business research, however, is not restricted to those approaches which are 'ideologically driven'. It is also to be found in much of the work that is empirically grounded. In this latter area, though, the oversimplification is generally the result of inadequate conceptualization in a more limited sense – namely, a reliance upon the assumption that there exists a homogeneous 'small firm sector' which can be comprehended by using a universal conception of the 'small business'.

The following chapters aim to demonstrate that the type of sociological approach developed above offers the prospect of a solution to these difficulties. In particular, the inherent flexibility and open-endedness of the structural formulations allow their adaptation to a wide range of empirical situations in a manner which does not reduce conceptualization to the level of a single, arbitrary dimension (such as, for example, 'size' or 'turnover'). This is now being recognized (Curran and Burrows 1989) as a possible solution to the persistent problem of definition that has plagued so much empirical small business research. It is thus a consideration of the empirical base of small business research that serves as the central theme of the next chapter.

Chapter two

The empirical investigation of UK small business

The question of definition is central to the empirical investigation of small business. It takes very little methodological under-standing to realize that the way in which the small firm is conceived will have profound implications for the validity and reliability of data generated. Even so, it would be charitable to describe the approach of researchers to this problem as cavalier. The result is, on the one hand, an almost total lack of consistency between definitions of the small firm, and, on the other hand, an overwhelming reliance upon arbitrary one-dimensional concepts.

But why should small business definition present such difficulty? This question can best be answered by looking at the pattern of small business definitions that has emerged in the UK since the influential Bolton Report (1971). Probably the most widely used definition of a small business is that based upon an upper 'ceiling' of 200 employees. This is commonly taken to be the definition used by Bolton, an association which has given it a certain authority. In fact, this particular criterion was intended only to apply to manufacturing businesses and was one of a number of definitions employed by the Bolton Committee. Not only this, the Committee, unlike many of its followers, was at least openly attentive to the weaknesses of definition. As it rightly noted, the root of the problem lay in the very diversity of small business:

Small firms are present in virtually every industry and the characteristics they share as small firms are sometimes not apparent because of the differences arising from the contrasting conditions of different industries. There is also extreme varia-tion ... as regards efficiency, methods of operation, the nature of the market served and the size of the resources employed. Thus, a manufacturing business employing up to 200 people has

very little in common with a small shop owned and run by a married couple.
(Bolton 1971:xv)

Indeed, it was to escape from this dilemma that the Committee constructed an 'economic definition' of the small firm based upon the three 'essential' characteristics of market share (which should be small), personalized management by the owner(s), and independence of ownership and operation (Bolton 1971:1). Despite worthy intentions, this turned out to be a case of 'out of the frying pan and into the fire'. Although it captured qualitatively the essence of small business, its criteria proved impossible to measure quantitatively because of the complexity of the data required and the dependence upon inherently ambiguous terms like 'relatively small', 'personalized way' and 'free from outside control'. Finally, the Committee fell back on a series of essentially arbitrary, one-dimensional definitions tailored to suit different industrial sectors. As can be seen from Table 2.1, the 'less than 200' definition was one among many.

Table 2.1 The small firm sector as defined by the Bolton Committee

Industry	Statistical definition
Manufacturing	200 employees or less
Retailing	£50,000 p.a. turnover or less
Wholesale trades	£200,000 p.a. turnover or less
Mining/quarrying	25 employees or less
Motor trades	£50,000 p.a. turnover or less
Construction	25 employees or less
Miscellaneous services	£50,000 p.a. turnover or less
Road transport	5 vehicles or less

Source: Adapted from Bolton 1971:3

What, then, are the weaknesses of such definitions that make them so unsatisfactory? The first problem is that the use of a single-measure criterion (e.g., number of employees, turnover, etc.) can obscure important aspects of the businesses being considered. It is difficult, for instance, to detect if the business is genuinely independent or a subsidiary of a larger organization. Similarly, it hides differences between firms within the definitional category, particularly if the definitional limit allows large internal variation (e.g., the 'fewer than 200' definition cannot distinguish between a business with two employees and one with 199). In practice such differences may be as great, if not greater, than those between some 'small' firms and excluded 'large' firms.

Then there is the question of appropriateness over time and across industries. On the one hand, definitions based on a single indicator are vulnerable to the effects of change. For example, those which define smallness on the basis of turnover or output per annum will clearly be affected by inflation, whilst those which use the number of workers cannot capture the seasonal or longer-term employment level fluctuations that characterize many small organizations. On the other hand, there is the very real danger that research findings based upon one definition of 'smallness' will, wittingly or unwittingly, be generalized to industrial sectors where this definition is inappropriate. The risk of dependence upon indiscriminately applied definitions is that studies which appear to be talking about the same thing often conceal conflicting results by subsuming important dimensions of variation within a single definitional criterion (e.g., size) which, in turn, is assumed to be the key independent variable (Hakim 1989a).

Finally, there is the problem of 'definitional multiplication', as researchers construct their own definitions to suit their own purposes which, in turn, confuses the interpretation of data-bases and heightens their inherent weaknesses. Cross (1983), for instance, provides a list of definitions in use in the UK in the early 1980s – a list which is by no means exhaustive (see Table 2.2).

The problem with this sort of multiplication of definitions is not merely one of confusion. All the definitions listed in Table 2.2 specify only an upper limit for the relevant category but make no mention of the lower limit. Whilst this is not a serious problem for the definition itself, it invariably creates practical difficulties, as most commonly used data-bases *do* set a lower limit which excludes very small firms. The Census of Production (which covers manufacturing industries), for example, specifically excludes firms with fewer than twenty workers, whereas the voluntary nature of VAT registration for businesses with a turnover of less than (currently) £21,300 a year biases this otherwise useful data-base against very small and new businesses (Ganguly and Bannock 1985). The same is true of the data from the Dunn and Bradstreet credit rating agency, which has been used in both the UK and the USA, as few very small firms require credit ratings (Storey and Johnson 1986). These factors can give rise to the sort of error described by Cross (1983) who cites two studies using the same definition of small business but concluding that there were either 2.3 million or 1.3 million such businesses, a direct result of using data-bases with different minimum exclusions.

Table 2.2 Definitions relating to government assistance

Type of assistance	Definition
European Investment Bank loans	500 employees
Proprietory company	50 employees
Employment Act exemptions	20 employees
Council for Small Industries in Rural Areas (CoSIRA) aid	20 employees (skilled)
Export award	200 employees
Export visits	200 employees
Employment subsidy	200 employees
Computer-aided production mgt	500 employees
Industrial liaison service	500 employees
Consultancy scheme	500 employees
Collaborative arrangements, (manufacturing)	200 employees
Manufacturing advisory service	1,000 employees
Companies Act disclosure exemption	£1 million p.a. turnover
Proprietory company	£1.3 million p.a. turnover
Value Added Tax registration	£15,000 p.a. turnover
Price code exemptions	£1 million (manufacturing) p.a. turnover
	£250,000 (distribution/services) p.a. turnover
	£100,000 (professions) p.a. turnover
Competition Act exemptions	£5 million p.a. turnover

Source: Adapted from Cross (1983:89)

Such universal and one-dimensional definitions, by concealing the heterogeneous nature of small business activity, are also partly responsible for an associated problem of small business research, namely the indiscriminate generalization of results derived from manufacturing to all other types of small business. Manufacturing firms, in fact, are a minority group, however they are counted. They employ only one-quarter of all employees, and this proportion rises to no more than 27 per cent among small firms with fewer than fifty employees. According to Hakim's (1989a) analysis of the MAS Business Line survey (see p. 40ff. below), for instance, the proportion of businesses with fewer than fifty employees in distribution is more than twice as high as for any other single category, including manufacturing (15 per cent). The latter, however, has the largest proportion of firms with twenty-five to forty-nine employees (24 per cent), distribution falling to 12 per cent for this size band. These figures clearly show the danger of taking manufacturing to be representative of other than 'larger' small firms. They also, of course, reveal how such unrepresentativeness can be 'concealed' by data-bases that 'exclude' smaller businesses. There is, it seems, no reason to expect small manufacturing firms to be representative of all small firms, particularly when, as Hakim (1989a:30) notes, 'they are outnumbered three to one by small firms in the service sector'.

Curran and Burrows (1989:11) have also called attention to the association between the inadequate conceptualization of small business and the neglect of the service sector. They, too, point to the spurious validity of universal quantitative definitions and suggest an 'alternative' conception that, like the sociological approach developed in the previous chapter, is empirically grounded and capable of capturing the 'lived cultures' of those who create and sustain the small enterprise in the various sectors of the economy.[1] This requires an approach which seeks to comprehend small business in terms of *substantial* social relations (that is, in terms of 'real relations of contact and interaction which occur between some designated population's members' [Curran and Burrows 1989:6–7]), whereas most small business empirical research has remained at the *formal* level (concerned with relations of similarity and 'nominalist links between those who have been taxonomically distinguished as members of some population or grouping'). In many ways what is being advocated in this 'alternative approach' is a return to the sort of 'economic definition' of a small business rejected by the Bolton Committee (see p. 30 above). The objective now is to explain *variations* in the articulation of the defining characteristics (i.e., market share, management style, and independence) between small businesses and small business owners at the individual, organizational and industrial levels. Thus, apart from encouraging a concern with the qualitative dimensions of small business, it also points to a reformulation of quantitative data so that size alone no longer appears as the central independent variable. Given the dearth of data relating to small business in the 1960s and 1970s, such a task was understandably unrealistic for most researchers on anything other than a very limited scale. The same is not true today, however, and attempts are now beginning to be made to use small business data in a more analytical and empirically meaningful way. The remainder of this chapter examines some of these attempts as they relate to recent national-level data-sets.

By combining different sets of figures it is estimated that there are approximately 1.75 million small businesses (i.e., employing fewer than 200 workers) in Britain (employing, very roughly, one-third of the workforce) and around 3 million self-employed (Cross 1983; Curran and Burrows 1988; Hakim 1988). Such figures tell little of the real nature of small business, however. To discover more it is necessary to disaggregate the data and rely upon the findings of discrete data-sets which, whilst often comprehensive in their own right, are not always strictly comparable because of differing methodological and conceptual assumptions.

A significant step in providing a statistically representative picture has been taken by Curran and Burrows (1988) through their analysis of the General Household Survey for the period 1979–84. This analysis distinguishes between small business owners (defined as those employing between one and twenty-four people) and the self-employed (those who work for themselves but employ nobody else directly). This yields a sample of 5,700 (1,700 small business owners and 3,900 self-employed) that is claimed to be nationally representative. The principal value of this survey is the light it throws on the social characteristics of those who run small businesses, coupled with the fact that it allows comparisons to be made between the characteristics of 'entrepreneurs' and those of the employed population generally (also covered by the GHS). It is also notable in its coverage of very small firms (often ignored by other large data-bases – e.g., census of production).

Drawing upon this data source it is possible to develop a reasonably comprehensive, although somewhat general, profile of British small business in the 1980s. In terms of relative position of the self-employed and small business owners within the labour force, Curran and Burrows (1988) point to a noticeable increase over the period 1979–84, from 8 per cent to over 12 per cent. Excluding the numerically small categories of farmers, self-employed professionals, and business owners with more than twenty-five employees, small business owners (i.e., those with fewer than twenty-five workers) have increased from 2 per cent to 2.4 per cent of the employed workforce, and self-employed workers (those with no employees) from 4 per cent to 7.5 per cent (Curran and Burrows 1988:11). It is clear that the expansion in the numbers of self-employed is responsible for the bulk of growth in small enterprises. In absolute terms, the number of self-employed has increased from about 2 million in 1981 to more than 3 million[2] in 1988, an average growth of 136,000 each year (Hakim 1989b:287). The reasons for this growth are not easily determined in any definitive sense although the Institute for Employment Research has identified four 'key factors' which, they claim, underlie the upward trend of the 1980s. First, there is the growth in demand for business services in a competitive market structure which appears to favour small enterprises. Second, an expansion in the subcontracting of services by the large firms operating in these competitive markets (as an alternative to 'internal' provision) has created growing opportunities for self-employed providers. Third, further opportunities have been created by a similar growth in subcontracting activity within the public sector as a result of public-spending restraints. Finally, the coincidence of the expansion of self-employment with the Conservative government's concerted efforts to promote enterprise and entrepreneurship (Hakim 1988; Chapter seven of this book).

Hakim (1988:428) reduces these factors to two central questions: whether there has been a change of strategy among employers towards sub-contracting to smaller firms and/or the self-employed; and whether the government is succeeding in creating a new 'enterprise culture' and a climate of opinion which encourages the entrepreneurial spirit and produces a positive public image for self-employed workers.

In respect of a change in employer strategies towards a greater use of subcontracting (Brenson 1985; Fevre 1987) and, hence, self-employed workers, some increase is apparent, but this seems less than spectacular (Employers' Labour Use Strategies survey 1987), although there are indications of an increasing incidence and intensity of use of self-employed workers, a trend that seems likely to continue into the 1990s. Employers' reasons for using self-employed labour in this respect tend to emphasize the need for greater workforce flexibility and reduced labour costs (Hakim 1988:438).

The impact of the 'enterprise culture' is even more difficult to detect accurately. Hakim (1988) points to the tendency for self-employment to run in families (see Chapter three) and to the likelihood that family socialization patterns will foster and re-inforce the ideology of the enterprise culture. However, in this respect it is uncertain to what extent the government's attempts to propagate enterprise actually create new entrepreneurs or merely reinforce tendencies that would have existed anyway. Similar doubts exist about the high priority which the self-employed and potential self-employed give to 'entrepreneurial' motives such as independence, economic self-advancement, and challenge (Hakim 1989b:289), particularly since such attitudes have been reported as characteristic of certain small business owners long before the notion of the enterprise culture gained in popularity (e.g., Bechhofer *et al.* 1974). Perhaps of more direct relevance in this matter is the research conducted by Blackburn and Curran (1989:16) into the attitudes of 16–19-year-olds, i.e., those whose formative years have been those of the Thatcher government. This survey was designed to determine the 'enterprise awareness' of young people and their attitude towards running a business. Its conclusions did reveal a relatively high level of enterprise consciousness but, interestingly, there was little indication that the respondents had fallen victim to 'enterprise fever'. In spite of the government and the media's favourable treatment of self-employment and small business ownership opportunities, they remained realistic about the difficulties and pitfalls of such a 'career'.

These two sets of factors – employer strategies and the effects of the enterprise ideology – have certainly played a part in bringing about the increase in self-employment, but they are not solely responsible. Attention also needs to be directed towards those who enter self-employment not as a positive choice, but as the result of necessity (e.g., redundancy or lack of alternative employment opportunities) and, according to Hakim (1988:437), such 'reluctant' or 'involuntary' entrants comprise about one-third of all those who become self-employed. It should also be remembered that not all self-employed workers are entrepreneurs in the conventional sense. Many are labour-only sub-contractors who, whilst classified as self-employed for tax and insurance purposes, are likely, in practice, to have more in common with employees than the small business owner. Others are self-employed only on a part-time basis or combine self-employment with another job as an employee (see Chapter five). It would thus be a mistake to interpret the growth in self-employment as an unambiguous indication of an upsurge in entrepreneurial activity. For many it appears to be an alternative to an employee job rather than a conscious attempt to own a small business. Taken together, therefore, it seems that the rapid expansion of self-employment characteristic of the early 1980s was the result of a combination of very different factors – economic, political and social – working in the same direction. It is clearly debatable whether this is indicative of a widespread change in attitudes and orientations, or merely a coincidental outcome of contingent processes that will adjust to less remarkable levels in future.

Apart from the numbers of small business owners and self-employed, however, the GHS data also reveal more detailed information. Behind the overall expansion in the numbers of self-employed and small business owners, for instance, the relative gender 'mix' over the 1979–84 period has remained stable at a ratio of three men to one woman (Curran and Burrows 1988:12). This exposes a significant under-representation of women compared to their participation in the economy as employees, which, according to the same GHS data, stands at around 44 per cent. Indeed, whilst both men and women have increased their participation in small business activity, the rate of increase for men (63 per cent) has been greater than that for women (47 per cent) (Curran and Burrows 1988:12; cf. Carter and Cannon 1988:566). A detailed analysis of women's position as small business owners is undertaken in Chapter three, and for the present it is necessary only to indicate the patterns of gender participation in small business activity. The details of the distribution by economic activity for male and female self-employed and small business owners is given in Table 2.3. Here it can be seen that in terms of economic involvement women are more likely than men to own a business in the service sector and, in fact, 90 per cent of female small business owners operate in this area (compared to 65 per cent of men). This would seem to coincide with stereotyped notions of 'women's work' and, of course, their unequal access to capital and marketable skills through education and employment (Goffee and Scase 1985:9ff. This is strikingly revealed in the figures for self-employment in construction (Table 2.3) where less than 2 per cent of female self-employed operate, compared to nearly 40 per cent of men (the very high figure for men in this area reflects the traditional use of the practice of labour-only subcontracting [Scase and Goffee 1982; Austin 1980]). There appears little difference, however, between male and female small business owners and self-employed in terms of age profiles. For both groups the GHS data show that self-employment is likely to occur at an earlier age than small business ownership, reflecting, in all likelihood, the

Table 2.3 Economic activity by Standard Industrial Classification for small business owners and self-employed (%), GHS 1981–4

	Self-employed All Years*		Small business owners All Years*	
	M	F	M	F
Agriculture, forest, fishing, energy and mineral extraction	3.6	2.9	2.1	0.7
Manufacturing	6.7	9.2	10.3	7.0
Construction	39.5	1.7	22.7	2.0
Distribution, hotels, catering and repairs	22.7	32.0	47.7	65.4
Transport and communications	8.2	1.8	5.5	3.0
Banking, finance, insurance	6.9	16.8	5.0	3.0
Other services	12.3	35.5	6.7	17.8
N =	2011	757	886	298

Source: Adapted from Curran and Burrows 1988:34–5
Note: * Distribution for figures aggregated over 1981–84.
Not all columns = 100 per cent.

higher level of investment, expertise and trading capacity required to establish a business that is capable of employing others (see Table 2.4). Another notable feature of the GHS data on age composition is the clear indication they give of the existence of an 'age launch window', when life-cycle factors, such as occupational experience, access to capital, and stable domestic responsibilities, appear to favour the development of a small business career (see Chapter three). From the present data this would seem to be between the early thirties and mid-forties (see Table 2.4).

Table 2.4 Small business owners, self-employed workers and employees: breakdown by gender and age, 1979–84 combined

Age	Small business owners		Self-employed workers		Employees	
	M %	F	M %	F	M %	F
16–24	3.5	2.3	9.6	9.1	19.3	22.3
25–34	21.9	22.5	26.9	29.6	23.4	20.3
35–44	33.0	35.7	28.4	26.2	21.3	22.9
45–54	23.4	21.4	19.2	18.9	18.9	20.4
55–60	9.5	11.4	8.0	8.5	10.6	9.8
61–65	5.0	4.1	4.0	2.9	4.6	2.6
66–	3.8	2.7	3.8	4.8	1.9	1.6
N =	1357	440	2825	1091	37660	29326

Source: Curran and Burrows (1988:16)
Note: Not all columns = 100 per cent.

In addition to age composition, the GHS also yields interesting information about the hours worked by small business owners and the self-employed. Most notably over 80 per cent of male small business owners worked more than forty hours per week, compared to under 17 per cent of employees (although the GHS figures do not include overtime for the latter). Female small business owners also work longer hours than employees, but to a lesser extent than their male counterparts: more than 66 per cent of the former work over forty hours per week, compared to only 4 per cent of the latter. The pattern is similar for the self-employed, with more hours being worked than employees but fewer than small business owners (Curran and Burrows 1988:67–8). It seems, therefore, that overworking (admittedly a very subjective term) amongst those in business for themselves, in whatever form, is commonplace and, in this sense, the idea of the 'workaholic' small business owner has some foundation.

However, despite this heavy workload Curran and Burrows find little in the GHS data to support the notion that working for yourself is especially health-threatening. This conclusion is, however, qualified by the methodological problems of self-reported health states used by the GHS, a caution which seems well founded in the light of a more rigorous study of stress amongst small business owner-managers (albeit with a much smaller sample) conducted by Lambshead and Levy (1989). This study reports small business owners as exhibiting consistently higher scores than a comparative group of corporate managers on occupational stress scales, having a greater propensity to think and behave in Type 'A' patterns[3] (associated with high risk of coronary heart disease), and suffering from higher levels of physical and mental ill-health.

It is, of course, a matter of some interest whether such long hours and potential exposure to stress result in higher levels of personal wealth creation. On this matter the GHS provides information only by means of proxy measures of material reward (due to the limited nature of the earnings data) such as ownership of cars and homes. With regard to the former, both small business owners and the self-employed appear better off than the working population, with small business owners doing better than the self-employed by a clear margin. Similarly for home ownership, both groups are markedly better off than the working population, although the self-employed are, again, behind the small business owners. Thus, although wealth creation is seldom given as the prime motivation for being in business there is no indication that the achievement of non-material goals involves a sacrifice of material rewards (Curran and Burrows 1988:83).

Even though all the findings of the GHS have not been discussed in detail in this chapter (data relating to social origins, education and ethnicity will be the subject of discussion in the following chapter), a vivid indication of the sheer heterogeneity of small business activity has already emerged. Thus, apart from its inherent interest, representativeness and detail, the GHS analysis seems likely to play a key role in the interpretation of results derived from smaller-scale investigations, providing, in effect, a bench-mark against which such results can be assessed. As its analysts point out, it has opened up a renewable source of high-quality information that should, in future, allow comprehensive longitudinal study of the people who run small enterprises in Britain in the 1980s and 1990s.

One limitation of the GHS data, however, is that they are concerned primarily with individual-level data rather than that which bears upon small business activity at the organizational, industrial or national economic levels. In this respect some of the gaps can be filled by information from two other notable surveys of small business: the MAS Business Line survey (Hakim 1989a), and the Small Business Research Trust's *Quarterly Survey of Small Business in Britain*.

The MAS Business Line survey consists of 2,000 telephone interviews with a stratified random sample of establishments with a business telephone line in Britain, using British Telecom's computerized Yellow Pages Business Telephone Directory as a sampling frame (agriculture, fishing and forestry industries are completely excluded). The definition of 'small' used by the survey is an establishment with 'fewer than fifty staff' and a business telephone line, of which there are a total of 1.5 million in Britain, 750,000 of these being independent firms and the remainder being branch offices of larger organizations. The details of incidence and characteristics of these small firms are given in Table 2.5.

Hakim's analysis of this comprehensive data leads her to suggest that three of the dimensions isolated – type of business (legal status), size, and premises/home-base – are crucially associated with small business performance in the form of business growth:

> No growth firms are typically unincorporated businesses (sole proprietorships or, less frequently, partnerships) that are home-based and employ only one or two people including the owner manager. In contrast, fast growth firms are typically incorporated businesses with larger workforces based in separate business premises. All other factors (such as region, location in a major city or elsewhere and so forth) are of minimal or no importance [as indicators of growth potential].
> (Hakim 1989a:37)

From the data in Table 2.5, therefore, it can be seen that potential 'no-growth' firms are clearly not an insignificant section of the small business population, a finding which has direct bearing upon one of the most contentious claims made about small business in the 1980s: namely, its potential to generate new jobs and contribute significantly to the reduction of unemployment. The job generation debate has two origins – one political, the other academic. These, however, have become increasingly confused as politicians have seized selectively upon pieces of academic research in an attempt to substantiate often vague and emotive claims of an ideological nature (for examples see Storey and Johnson 1986). Indeed, contrary to many 'policy' statements, which proclaim small firms as a major source of job generation, a

Table 2.5 Incidence and characteristics of small, independent establishments with under fifty full-time workers

	Independent firms as % of group	All 1–50 workers	1–24 workers	25–49 workers	Independent firms N=100%	1–24 workers	25–49 workers
All independent estabs in Britain with up to 50 workers	65	100	100	100	747,970	96	4
No. of people employed full-time at estabs							
0–2	73	49	50	–	366,120	100	–
3–4	67	18	19	–	134,780	100	–
5–9	54	17	18	–	127,510	100	–
10–24	54	12	13	–	90,820	100	–
25–49	48	4	–	–	28,750	–	100
All under 25	65	96	100	–	719,220	100	–
All 25–49	48	4	–	100	28,750	–	100
Age of business							
1977: 11+ years	69	50	49	79	376,770	94	6
1978–81: 6–10 years	75	13	13	7	96,570	98	2
1982–85: 2–6 years	70	21	21	10	150,040	98	2
1986–88: up to 2–5 years	73	16	17	4	124,590	99	1
Type of business							
Gvt dependency (e.g. GP)	82	5	5	14	38,010	90	10
Limited Company	44	27	26	66	196,360	91	9
Partnership	71	17	18	5	127,620	99	1
Sole trader	85	47	49	10	350,260	99	1
Other (e.g. charities, clubs)	43	4	4	6	35,730	94	6
Home-based firm	76	34	35	12	250,000	99	1
Separate workplace	60	66	65	88	500,000	95	5
Sex of owner-manager							
Male	64	71	71	75	518,430	96	4
Female	64	29	29	25	211,680	97	3
Industry							
Mining, construction, etc.	82	11	12	13	84,070	96	4
Manufacturing	75	15	15	24	113,760	94	6
Distribution	62	34	34	12	251,480	99	1
Gvt health service	71	9	8	17	64,850	93	7
Business services, finance	45	8	8	10	58,090	95	5
Personal services	61	15	15	10	113,010	98	2
Transport, utilities	67	5	4	15	32,840	87	13
Other, don't know	68	4	4	–	29,880	100	–
Location:							
major cities	62	31	31	45	231,650	95	5
other	66	69	69	55	516,330	97	3
Region:							
North	67	36	36	17	267,340	98	2
Midlands	65	22	22	15	161,280	97	3
South	63	43	42	68	319,350	94	6

Source: Hakim 1989a:33

careful reading of the available evidence shows a much more equivocal and uncertain picture.

The job generation potential of small business was forced into the limelight by the work of Birch (1979) who, on the basis of a large-scale study of the manufacturing and service sectors in the USA between 1969 and 1976, claimed that 66 per cent of net new jobs were created by small firms employing fewer than twenty people. Whilst these findings were hailed with enthusiasm by proponents of small business, confusion over the precise definitions of the terms employed by Birch has resulted in much misrepresentation of his results (for an account of some of these see Storey 1982). Equally unfortunately, enthusiasm over these apparently startling results has led many commentators to ignore the not insignificant methodological difficulties associated with Birch's work.[4]

Gallagher and Stewart (1985), for example, claimed that 31 per cent of gross new jobs in the UK private sector between 1971 and 1981 were created in the small business sector, although Storey and Johnson (1986), having subjected these latter findings to a rigorous critique, concluded that even the 31 per cent figure was likely to have been optimistic. Later research by Storey and associates (1987) suggests that the majority of new jobs are created by a very few firms and that such jobs are frequently qualitatively distinct from those which have been lost, often being less skilled and more frequently filled by part-time women workers. Storey, in particular, has been critical of government support for small firms justified on the grounds that small business in general is an efficient creator of employment in the short term. His argument is that only a relatively few small businesses actually create employment on anything like a significant scale and that even these 'fast-growth' firms will contribute only marginally to employment growth in anything other than the long term. In practice, he suggests, employment will remain heavily conditioned by changes made by large enterprises, citing evidence from Cleveland (Storey 1982:209) to support his case: 'This [local] economy created less than 2,000 new manufacturing jobs in wholly new surviving firms over an eleven year period. In one day in 1980 the British Steel Corporation announced that, because of the world recession, output had to be cut and 3,000 jobs would be lost from the Cleveland area.' The Cleveland research and later studies by Storey and colleagues (e.g., Storey 1985; Storey *et al.* 1987) have resulted in the suggestion that government aid to small firms should be targeted at those which have a good chance of fast long-term growth and, hence, provide conditions for efficient job generation (see Chapter seven). Here again, Hakim's analysis of the Business Line data is relevant, as this suggests that there would be great difficulty in predicting fast-growth firms. Whilst it is possible to say what a fast-growth firm is *likely* to look like, the discriminatory variables are not exclusive to fast growth-firms, making a priori identification distinctly problematic. This leads Hakim (1989a) to question the feasibility of 'picking the winners' on operational and empirical grounds, for although certain characteristics are more common among fast-growth firms, a proportion of no-growth firms display the same features. This means that either the 'selection process' will remain uncertain, or it will demand such heavy resourcing (to overcome the poor predictive power of the discriminatory variables) as to outweigh potential benefits.

A less contentious angle on small business growth and performance is provided by the *Quarterly Survey of Small Business in Britain*.[5] This survey, started in 1984, collects data on a variety of small business issues from a sample of the members of three organizations representing small business interests: The National Federation of Self-Employed, The Association of Independent Businesses, and The Forum of Private Business. This usually results in between 1,000 and 2,000 responses. Each survey reports on changes in sales and employment and the most important problems faced by small businesses. In addition, each issue of the survey covers one or more special topics (these have included the use of computers, exports, telecommunications products, government policy, skill shortages and business expansion – for an index see vol. 4, 4, 1989).

Turning first to the problems reported by the small business owners interviewed for the SBRT *Quarterly Survey*, it seems that between 1984 and 1988 small business has acted as a fairly accurate barometer of problems in the economy generally. Thus, 'finance and interest rates' consistently represented the principal source of concern for small business owners, increasingly so in recent years, followed in the early 1980s by 'total tax burden' and 'lack of business'. Whilst in 1988 'shortage of skilled employees' moved into fairly clear second place, in 1989 it was displaced to fourth place by 'total tax burden'. In the 1989 figures the per cent mention of inflation doubled from 2.8 to 5.6 (Table 2.6).

Certainly until 1989 the performance of small business reported by the *Quarterly Survey* appeared generally healthy, as shown in Table 2.7.[6] In fact, the survey for the fourth quarter of 1988 showed the number of respondents expanding both sales and employment outnumbering those declining (in both sales and

Table 2.6 Problems experienced by respondents of *Quarterly Survey*, per cent mentions 1984–9/1

	1984	1985	1986	1987	1988	1989*
Finance and interest rates	17.1	24.0	25.0	18.0	25.5	27.4
Total tax burden	15.9	16.6	17.7	21.3	12.5	14.6
Competition from big business	12.0	11.1	11.8	12.5	10.4	5.1
Lack of skilled employees	5.4	5.6	7.2	11.1	16.9	13.1
Low turnover or lack of business	15.3	15.7	14.7	13.0	8.7	3.0
Government regulations or paperwork	12.6	10.2	6.8	6.3	6.0	7.3
High rates of pay	4.2	2.0	1.3	1.3	1.3	0.7
Inflation	3.5	2.2	1.1	1.1	2.8	5.6
Shortage of materials	0.9	0.9	1.3	1.3	3.3	0.3
Other	10.9	9.2	10.0	9.6	10.6	14.5
No response	1.4	2.0	3.1	4.5	1.9	8.4

Source: SBRT 1988: 18; SBRT 1989:9
Note: * Figures for first quarter only.

Table 2.7 Changes in turnover and employment by 'balance', 1986–8

	Changes on year			
	1987/4 on 1986/4	1988/1 on 1987/1	1988/2 on 1987/2	1988/3 on 1987/3
	Sales Turnover			
All Businesses				
Up	65.1	65.3	68.3	67.4
Down	12.4	13.0	13.3	12.5
Same	20.4	17.7	15.9	17.4
No response	2.1	3.6	2.5	2.7
Total	100.0	99.6	100.0	100.0
Balance	+52.7	+52.3	+55.0	+54.9
	Employment			
All businesses				
Up	32.3	28.5	31.0	30.7
Down	8.9	9.2	9.0	8.4
Same	52.5	53.4	51.4	52.0
No response	6.3	8.9	8.6	8.8
Total	100.0	100.0	100.0	99.9
Balance	+23.4	+19.3	+22.0	+22.3
Base	1042	933	983	950

Source: SBRT (1988) 4, 4: 7

employment) by eight to one. With the increasing inflation and interest rates of 1989, however, the prospect looks less rosy, with both growth and employment falling more than expected, a reduction in the number of expanding companies, and a slowing in growth of those still expanding (SBRT 1988, 4, 4:2). Indeed, other commentators such as the CBI's Small Business Council and the credit agency Dunn and Bradstreet are painting a bleak picture for small business in the 1990s as liquidations total 10,500 or more for 1989 compared to 9,700 in 1988. Thus, according to Irving (1989): 'when interest rates are high, corporate customers – which are often rich in cash – hold off payments to their small suppliers for as long as they possibly can. When they do pay up, it is often too late to save the struggling small man [sic] from the liquidator.'

Looked at across the 1980s, therefore, it would seem that small business activity is closely tied to the fortunes of the wider economy and that small firms are extremely sensitive to economic changes. If the high interest rates and rising inflation that have characterized the UK economy in the closing years of the 1980s continue, there must be real fears for the continued expansion of small business on the scale seen earlier in the decade. Indeed, it may be that whereas workers were the principal casualties of the recession of the early 1980s, small business owners and the self-employed will be those of the 1990s. In an economic downturn that has come at the end of a period of particularly rapid expansion, increasing numbers of small firms will find it progressively more difficult to meet repayments on loans taken out when borrowing was cheap and order-books buoyant. Similarly, and not a little ironically, many self-employed may fall victim to 'leaner and fitter' large businesses now able to take advantage of the greater flexibility afforded by the use of subcontractors rather than direct labour, as service contracts are terminated or 'renegotiated'. To what extent the Enterprise Culture ideology can endure such a buffeting is a matter for debate, as is the extent to which it can sustain the current fashionability of small business in drastically changed economic conditions. Of greater importance than the fate of a political dogma, however, is the effect that such economic conditions will have upon established small business and upon small business formation in the future. In part this will be determined by changes in the structure of the economy and their impact upon different industries and organizations. But also of importance will be individuals' perceptions and definitions of these changes and their willingness and ability to act upon them. And to appreciate this it is necessary to know more about those who become small business proprietors and their reasons for so doing.

The arguments and data presented earlier in this chapter have already pointed to both a considerable degree of heterogeneity in this respect, and the utility of conceiving small business as an active 'process' rather than as an arbitrary statistical category. The next chapter expands upon these ideas in greater detail, exploring the 'substantial' social relationships of entrepreneurs and entrepreneurship.

Chapter three

Small business and the entrepreneur

As with so many notions in small business investigation, there is no commonly agreed understanding as to precisely what characteristics, attitudes and behaviours are indicative of entrepreneurial activity. The result, invariably, has been confusion, as writers have either used the concept in a vague and unspecified manner, as a convenient alternative to 'small business owner', or have constructed definitions of an extremely specific and restricted nature. In consequence there is frequently an uncomfortable degree of slippage between these two understandings, whereby all small business owners are indiscriminately and automatically ascribed the qualities of innovation, creativity and risk-hunger (the usual elements of more specific definitions) regardless of the real nature of their activity.

Of those who specify rigorous conditions for the identification of entrepreneurial behaviour Drucker (1985:36) is perhaps the most thorough. For him, entrepreneurship is not inextricably linked to small business or new business as such, but rather to the nature of business activity. To be entrepreneurial, an enterprise has to create something new, something different, to change or transmute values. Therefore, the entrepreneurial business must, amongst other things, be expansive as it develops new areas and creates new markets. But it will be recalled from the previous chapter, no-growth or stable-state small firms can be expected easily to outnumber fast-growth small businesses. Using Drucker's criteria, then, few UK small business owners would merit the title of entrepreneur, as most operate in well-tried areas of the economy, serve markets that already exist in a manner that mirrors established businesses, and adopt modes of organization that are traditional rather than innovative. As Storey (1982:1) has pointed out, 'For every boffin businessman [sic], intending to manufacture and market a wholly new and technically sophisticated product, there are scores of insurance agents, garage mechanics, hairdressers and carpenters who begin in business providing very familiar goods and services.'

Whilst Drucker's restricted usage has precision on its side, the 'looser' formulation can call upon pragmatism. The understanding which associates the entrepreneur with the owner-manager of *any* new and/or small business has become so established in both popular and academic discourse that to challenge this meaning would be likely simply to add to the confusion that already exists. It seems preferable, therefore, for the term to be used in its loosest form (i.e., as a synonym for the small business owner in general) but to specify particular *types* of entrepreneurial activity (e.g., technological entrepreneurship) as and when appropriate. This has the additional benefit of ensuring that the practice of entrepreneurial activity is conceived as being located in relation to other social practices and environments (i.e., which define the 'type') rather than treated as some unique and privileged quality of the individual. This usage will be adopted in the following pages, where it will become apparent that the explicit specification of types of entrepreneurial activity is a necessary precondition for the adequate comprehension of the diverse motives and actions of small business owners.

However, the problematic nature of the concept of entrepreneurship has only relatively recently become a subject for critical attention. Certainly in terms of published output, the bulk of work in this field has concerned the grail-like search to discover precisely those universal psychological attributes that can identify the 'entrepreneurial personality'. Underlying this quest has generally been the assumption that entrepreneurial behaviour is primarily a function of an individual's personality traits rather than a direct response to social environment. In other words, whilst social experience cannot be discounted, (particularly that associated with early childhood), it is of interest only to the extent that it can be seen to shape the individual personality.

Kets de Vries (1977), for example, points to early family experiences as a key factor in forming a personality that will, in later life, dispose the individual towards entrepreneurial behaviour. In particular, images of endured hardships are supposed to leave the adult troubled by a burdensome psychological inheritance, leading to problems of self-esteem and insecurity which, in turn, result in repressed aggression towards persons in control (Chell 1986:103). The result, apparently, is that the entrepreneur, driven by distrust and suspicion of those in authority, searches for 'non-structured situations where he can assert his control and independence' (Kets de Vries 1977:49 sic). In consequence it is extremely hard, if not impossible, for individuals with an entrepreneurial disposition to integrate their personal needs with those of organizations. 'To design one's own organisation ... often becomes the only alternative.'

Another well-known attempt to investigate the entrepreneurial personality is that of McClelland (1961). For McClelland entrepreneurial activity – equated roughly with the ability individually to accumulate wealth via intervention in the means of economic production and trade[1] – is positively associated with the psychological characteristic of *need achievement* (or n-Ach as it has become known). McClelland concluded, on the basis of historical and cross-cultural studies, that economic growth was related to the frequency with which achievement themes appeared in popular stories and literature, particularly that intended for children; in particular he suggested that a high level of achievement imagery in children's stories would manifest itself in a period of economic growth some thirty years later, i.e., when the children were economically active adults.

The principal psychological factor involved in the generation of high achievement motivation was, in McClelland's view, parental treatment.[2] Mothers of high-achievers apparently expected their sons to be capable of self-reliant and independent action at an early age and placed relatively few restrictions on their actions, except to discourage childish dependent behaviour; neither did fathers seek to dominate their sons. Conversely, children who felt rejected by their mothers tended to be low in achievement motivation.

The apparent contradiction with Kets de Vries notwithstanding, the notion that high achievement motivation is associated with entrepreneurial activity has received some support from later studies. But this support must be qualified by the fact that whilst important, it has not proved possible to isolate achievement motivation unequivocally as the single most important characteristic of the entrepreneurial personality. Other studies have added characteristics such as veridical perception (roughly, realism), anxiety or neuroticism (Lynn 1969), support, independence and leadership (Hornaday and Aboud 1971). In fact some writers (e.g., Hornaday and Bunker 1970; Timmons *et al.* 1977) have suggested that at least twenty different personality characteristics can be shown to discriminate between entrepreneurs and others.

This type of disagreement between research findings over the salience of particular personality characteristics is indicative of more general difficulties associated with this kind of personality-based theory. To begin with, the direction of causality between trait-inspired behaviour and its effects upon the social world is difficult to establish. Remember McClelland's argument that patterns of child-rearing give rise to personality traits which lead individuals to contribute to society-wide economic growth and expansion. It could equally well be argued that changes in economic conditions stimulate and facilitate particular patterns of familial and wealth-creating behaviours in individuals. In other words, the direction of causality is reversed: it is not personality variables that shape the economic world but, on the contrary, conditions in the economic world which allow the development of particular personality types and associated patterns of behaviour. If this is the case then the search for the roots of entrepreneurship in the make-up of the individual personality is misguided, as it would merely be confronting effect rather than cause.

Additionally, the very notion of personality traits as the basis for a theory of social action is susceptible to the criticism that such traits are difficult to define and to measure, and entail an over-simplified model of the individual (Argyle and Little 1972; Mischel 1981).

Liles (1981), for example, argues that whilst personality factors may provide necessary conditions for entrepreneurial success they are not sufficient. He combines life-cycle factors with an 'exchange' or 'balance' conception of motivation to explain individual entrepreneurial activity. Certain periods in the life-cycle, Liles suggests, are more amenable to entrepreneurship than others. In particular, the individual must perceive himself (again, this model is based upon males) as possessing the capacity to start a business, a perception which is likely to be strongly affected by previous work experience and career stages; experientially the individual must be 'ready'. Against such 'readiness', however, must be set a number of 'restraints', such as perceived risk in relation to possible returns. In this respect the perception of risk is also related to life-cycle factors, especially those associated with family and domestic responsibilities. Liles suggests that in the life-cycle of the would-be entrepreneur there is a period – roughly five years either side of thirty – which presents itself as a 'window of opportunity' for entrepreneurial activity (see Chapter two of this book). This is a 'free-choice' period during which the balance of capacities and restraints is relatively favourable; outside this period restraints are likely to outweigh capacities (Liles 1981:33ff).

This notion of a balance of restraints and capacities is extended, in slightly different terms, by Cromie (1987:44), who talks of multiple determinants of entrepreneurship, which include the individual's motives, experience in the incubator (last employment before founding) job, career experience, entrepreneurial skill, information available, and labour market considerations. Indeed, the greater awareness of diversity among small businesses has stimulated a move towards more complex models of entrepreneurial behaviour, placing greater emphasis on the integration of social and psychological factors and the contingent nature of their interaction.

Recent research into the influence of family background upon entrepreneurial propensities, for instance, has concentrated less upon its questionable effect as ultimate determinant of personality disposition, and more upon its role in the provision of access to resources – social and material – that facilitate or constrain entrepreneurial activity.

There have been several sociological studies, for instance, that have suggested links between socio-economic status – in particular, father's occupation – and small business activity. Most evidence suggests that, in numerical terms, the bulk of small business proprietors are drawn from families located in the lower-middle strata of society, i.e., skilled manual workers, supervisors and routine white-collar employees and from families already involved in some kind of small business activity (Boswell 1973). Whilst this pattern of distribution has been more or less uncontested, the interpretation of its significance has been called into question by Curran and Burrows (1988).

The conventional view has always been to assume that entry into small business is principally a means of upward social mobility for members of the lower-middle social strata alluded to above. Aldrich *et al.* (1986), for example, found, on the basis of a study of 149 shopkeepers in three major cities in England, that 60 per cent of the sample had fathers who were in manual occupations. Similarly, Scase and Goffee (1987) have claimed that entrepreneurship in Western countries has enabled the socially disadvantaged to achieve material and personal success by offering an alternative to career mobility in large-scale organizations. In short, 'entrepreneurship offers alternative routes for those who, without academic, professional or technical qualifications are excluded from meritocratic achievement' (Scase and Goffee 1987:8). Maya (1987:51) supports such a view with data from France to show that 'artisanal small business' (i.e., based upon manual craft skills) increasingly functions 'as a channel of upward mobility giving members of the working class access to the middle classes'.

Curran and Burrows's (1988) analysis does not dispute the fact that lower/middle levels of society are important 'feeder strata' for small business ownership and self-employment. In fact their data reveals that among small business owners (those with between one

51

and twenty-four employees) the skilled manual and routine white-collar categories supplied just over 37 per cent of the total for the period 1979–84, the equivalent figure for the self-employed (independent business owners without employees) being just over 40 per cent. Both figures, as they remark, represent substantial proportions, but whereas most previous analyses have stopped at this point, Curran and Burrows (1988:29) take their argument a stage further and compare the backgrounds of those entering small business with those of all employees in the GHS. The result is that the representation of individuals from the lower-middle strata in small business now appears lower than that amongst all employees, where 46 per cent come from such a background. So although those from skilled manual, routine white-collar and supervisory socio-economic backgrounds are numerically significant, proportionately these two groupings supply less to the small enterprise-owning strata than they do to the employee population as a whole. On the other hand, though, children of the employer/manager and professional strata are more than proportionately represented, which supports an interpretation that rather than an avenue of upward social mobility for lower social strata, small business ownership is better viewed as a 'catch net' for the downwardly mobile (see Table 3.1).

Table 3.1 Small business owners' socio-economic background: GHS 1979–84 (percentage)

SEG of father	1979 M	F	1980 M	F	1981 M	F	1982 M	F	1983 M	F	1984 M	F	Employees* M	F
Employer/ Manager	27	21	27	34	33	25	33	29	38	21	28	33	15	16
Professional	3	2	3	3	1	4	3	4	5	4	2	4	3	4
Self-employed non-prof.	8	5	5	3	5	2	7	3	4	2	7	4	4	5
Routine white collar & supers.	10	15	9	9	12	19	14	4	19	19	18	16	17	14
Skilled manual	25	33	26	28	24	31	17	21	14	23	19	22	30	31
Semi & unskilled manual	15	10	17	13	11	10	12	19	12	9	9	8	20	20
Other	11	15	12	9	14	9	14	16	8	15	17	14	10	11
N =	175	61	168	32	130	52	152	48	151	56	163	51	22648	17316

Source: Curran and Burrows 1988: 25
Note: * Figures for all employees under 50 years of age aggregated over 1979–84. Not all columns = 100 per cent.

Unfortunately Curran and Burrows's data do not indicate whether different social groups are associated with different forms of small business. Perhaps not surprisingly, Maya's (1987:51) French findings suggest that artisanal small business is the preferred means of achievement for those from the manual working class, whereas shopkeeping is more likely to serve as 'a net which cushions the fall of the skidders and the superannuated of both the higher middle class and the grande bourgeoisie'. Whilst the data are not yet available to confirm this, there seems little reason to suspect that similar patterns of business 'self-selection' by social class will not also characterize the UK.

It is interesting to speculate further whether the recent boom in small business ownership, rather than representing the flowering of opportunities for those without conventional credentials or the extension of social progress through individual merit and achievement, might become instead another area which is progressively 'annexed' and 'closed' (Parkin 1979) by members of the dominant classes, safeguarding the benefits it can yield for their own offspring. Indeed, it could be suggested that the multiplication of small business courses and the concern of business-interest groups in greater 'professionalism' in small business management represent the first stages in an attempt to erect exclusionary credentialist boundaries. A recent evaluation of the Loan Guarantee Scheme (Ridyard *et al.* 1989:421; see also Chapter seven), for example, came to the conclusion that this could be made more reliable by 'insisting that applicants have formal training in business skills . . . [and advocating] improved appraisal of business plans, monitoring, and training in business skills'. And, as Parkin has observed of the process of 'social closure' via credentialism,

> Formal qualifications and certificates would appear to be a handy device for ensuring that those who possess 'cultural capital' are given the best opportunity to transmit the benefits of professional status to their own children. Credentials are usually supplied on the basis of tests designed to measure certain class-related qualities and attributes.
> (Parkin 1979:55)

The worry is not that members of lower social strata will be formally precluded from small business ownership (although this may be the indirect effect if, for example, institutional lenders begin to insist upon the possession of a 'small business qualification' as a sign of loan-worthiness, or if government regulates to ensure that only 'qualified' practitioners can operate in certain areas) but rather that the growing aura of 'professionalism' and 'managerialism' will make the owner-manager role appear unamenable to those who have failed in early life to internalize these particular values (cf Kets de Vries 1977).

At present, however, this does not seem to be an immediate threat. Curran and Burrows's data on the educational attainments of small business owners and the self-employed indicate that in terms of the highest academic qualifications obtained there is a lower level of attainment than for employees generally, particularly in terms of higher educational qualifications (e.g., university or polytechnic degrees). In fact, 'those who run their own businesses or who are self employed are less frequently drawn from the ranks of those with the highest formal qualifications than would be expected from the proportion of degree holders in the population as a whole' (Curran and Burrows 1988:47). (As will be seen later, this picture is somewhat complicated when these results are broken down by gender.)

But in terms of 'non-academic' qualifications, and particularly apprenticeships, the GHS data do support the notion of the 'artisan entrepreneur' who starts a business on the basis of craft training and skills, particularly for men. The proportion of male small business owners and self-employed holding apprenticeships as their highest qualification is higher than amongst employees generally – 15 per cent as opposed to 9 per cent (Curran and Burrows 1988:52).

Overall, however, whilst these latest data tend to support long-held beliefs that small business owners are generally poorly qualified (Boswell 1973; Bolton 1971), the patterns which do emerge are of slight rather than striking differences, and in qualitative terms the picture is distinctly mixed (Storey 1982). Thus neither lack nor possession of educational qualifications would seem to be an undue hindrance in starting a business, although there is some evidence to suggest that possession of a degree (or equivalent) may lead to better business performance (Gudgin and Fothergill 1979).

To summarize the argument so far, it appears that small business ownership is more accessible to those from higher socio-economic classes than those from lower strata, but such access is by no means exclusive, and large numbers of the latter classes manage to become business owners. In terms of education, small business owners tend not to be overly well-qualified and it is plausible that this can represent an alternative career route for those without formal 'credentials'. Indeed, such a view would be supported by those who suggest that the entre-preneurial personality is characterized by a strong need to achieve and a simultaneous rejection of conventional authority structures.

As an explanation of the reasons for an individual becoming a small business owner, however, this remains incomplete. It has taken no real account of the views, definitions and meanings which small business owners themselves use to explain their actions. In this respect, considerable importance is often attached to recent occupational/employment experiences.

These experiences can be grouped into one of two broad patterns of influence which, for analytical purposes, may be distinguished as 'formative' and 'reactive' respectively. Formative influence refers to those situations where the work experience of an individual provides that person, as a matter of course, with the skills and abilities necessary to make starting a business appear a viable and attainable possibility. These skills and abilities may be of many kinds, either practical, managerial, financial, attitudinal or a combination of all.

If formative influence is exerted in a positive direction – by opening a 'window of opportunity' or by building business competence – reactive influence arises from negative experiences. It represents a rejection of, or escape from, a situation regarded as intolerable and/or unfulfilling. Small business ownership, in this case, represents a means of escape from unsatisfactory work experiences.

Regarding formative influence, a great deal of attention has been devoted to the notion of small businesses as effective 'incubators' of entrepreneurship amongst employees. Small firms, it is claimed, provide a work experience which equips the employee with the skills and attitudes necessary to found his or her own enterprise. This is supposed to include direct exposure to risk and a sense of responsibility for commercial success as a result of being 'in touch' with all aspects of the organization, a totality of knowledge that also allows individuals to determine, in advance, the means by which their ideas may be translated into entrepreneurial action (Coyne and Binks 1983:33). This point is made in slightly different terms by Storey (1982), who quotes his reply to the House of Lords Select Committee on Unemployment:

If you work in a relatively small firm employing, let us say, less than ten people, the probability is that if you have enough managerial talent you will see the whole operation through from the beginning to the end; in other words, you will sweep the floor, you will do the accounts, you will do the buying, you will do the company marketing, public relations and might even lend a hand on the production side. That means you are in a much better position, you are better trained, to establish your own firm, because you have seen the job through as a comprehensive exercise.

(Storey 1982:93–4)

Scase and Goffee's (1982:224) study of small business owners in the building industry reveals evidence of a similar kind, where small employers sometimes provide practical 'start-up assistance' to certain of their employees, usually in the form of 'loans' of capital equipment and materials for the purposes of spare-time work, thereby allowing employees to 'trade' autonomously and obtain experience of 'quasi-self-employment'. It should be remembered, of course, that such formative influences will not affect all workers in small firms equally. Storey (1982), in fact, seems to refer to those who occupy managerial positions but, as he acknowledges, many of the managerial functions described may be unavailable to employees, being the sole prerogative of the owner (Goss 1986). Indeed, some workers in small firms may be denied such experience precisely because it might equip them to leave and start a business in competition with their original employer.

The fact that many small business founders are former small business workers might, in this light, equally well be explained by reference to reactive rather than formative influences. If, as will be seen in Chapter four, small firms offer fewer promotion prospects, less job security and lower wages, then to start one's own business may be the only means of escaping such conditions, particularly if better employment in a large enterprise is not a viable alternative. Stanworth and Curran (1979), for instance, argue that those who begin their working lives in small businesses tend to be relatively poorly qualified and soon develop a history of job instability, factors which are viewed unfavourably by large enterprises. The result is that they become 'trapped' in a secondary labour market, their only employment choices being to continue working for small firms or to start their own business.

Instances of reactive influences upon the decision to commence in business are, indeed, well documented. Bechhofer *et al.* (1974:121) make this point in relation to their Edinburgh shopkeepers, for many of whom owning a small business was seen as an escape from the alienation of the manual workers' world and as a relief from hierarchical authority. This reaffirms Chinoy's (1955) earlier study of automobile workers in the USA, where small business offered an alternative to increasingly mechanized and deskilled factory labour, and finds an echo in the author's own research (Goss 1986; 1989) in the printing industry. Here were found several cases of printers starting businesses in response to the perceived threat posed by new technology to their skills and self-identity as craftsmen; in some cases they were prepared to sacrifice the long-term profitability and prospects of their new businesses to preserve 'old' technology and traditional working practices.

Similar motives were reported among builders by Scase and Goffee (1982:72): 'Many respondents had decided to become self-employed because of a wish to exercise greater control over their immediate work tasks. Indeed, their decisions may be seen as the outcome of an essential tension which confronts many craftsmen in modern capitalist enterprises.' More recently, these same authors have suggested that greater employer control and closer monitoring of performance may spur increasing numbers of managerial employees to become entrepreneurs as a means of enhancing self-fulfilment and job satisfaction (Scase and Goffee 1987).

Finally, using data from Northern Ireland, Cromie (1987) found that job dissatisfaction ranked equal second as a reason given by founders of small firms for establishing their enterprises, the level of dissatisfaction being greater than would normally be expected. (The first reason given was the not unrelated desire for greater autonomy.)

The previous occupational experiences of owner-managers not only influence the decision to start a business, they frequently affect the individual more deeply. They may become an integral part of that person's 'self-identity' and, as such, extend into the everyday conduct of the business itself. Using what they describe as a 'social action' model (see Chapter one of this book), Stanworth and Curran (1981:160) identify three entrepreneurial 'latent social identities', each of which represents a 'constellation of meanings ... which form the core of the entrepreneur's self-definition of the entrepreneurial role'. They outline these identities as follows:

1. *The artisan identity* Here the entrepreneurial role centres around intrinsic satisfactions of which the most important are personal autonomy at work, being able to pick the persons you work with, status within the workplace and satisfaction at producing a quality product backed with personal service ....
2. *The 'classical entrepreneur' identity* This latent social identity most closely resembles the classical economists' view of entrepreneurship. Earnings and profit become a core component in the entrepreneur's definition of his role and hence in the way he acts out his role ....

3. *The 'manager' identity* Here the entrepreneurial latent social identity centres on meanings and goals concerned with the recognition, by significant others, of managerial excellence. The entrepreneur structures his role performance to achieve this recognition from fellow members of the firm but, and more especially, from outsiders such as other businessmen.
(Stanworth and Curran 1981:161)

A similar point has been made by the author (Goss 1989), who distinguishes between two dimensions of the owner-manager role, both of which are experientially based and impinge upon the style and character of business activity. These dimensions – 'managerial orientation' and 'vocational attachment'[3] – are used to describe four distinct types of owner-manager proprietorial style: 'traditional', 'technocentric', 'marketeering', and 'isolationist'.

The *traditional* style, characterized by a high level of vocational attachment but a negative managerial orientation, is essentially similar to Stanworth and Curran's (1981) 'artisan identity', founded on the time-honoured practices of a particular occupation, the application of which gives meaning to business activity. The success of the business is a means to an end rather than an end in itself.

Technocentric proprietors combine a strong attachment to vocationalism with high managerial orientation. In relation to the former, this attachment is not to a static tradition but, rather, to the 'potential' to develop a given industrial process beyond its present boundaries. The direction of such development, however, is determined not by technical considerations alone but also by predictions of market opportunities, future innovations and long term business prospects.

For *marketeers*, business goals are, essentially, ends in themselves. As such the nature of the business in technical or vocational terms is less important than its ability to yield a regular profit. It is the market, rather than the nature of the product, that determines business policy and, unlike the technocentric style, it can be 'satisfied' at any technical price: managerial orientation is well developed but with low vocational attachment.

The *isolationist* style is characterized by a low managerial orientation and limited attachment to vocational aspirations. In effect, it represents a form of individual escapism from the conventional pressures of a market economy. Thus, business activity is not geared to profits or expansion but simply to the maintenance of an individually acceptable lifestyle. Similarly, the nature of the business is relatively unimportant in itself – it is not a significant source of identity or meaning. The motivation to remain in business is likely to lie in a combination of less attractive alternative opportunities elsewhere and the ability of proprietorship to enable greater satisfaction of non-work life chances. Thus, both vocational and managerial considerations are treated with narrow instrumentality.

The utility of typologies of this sort is twofold. In the first place they draw attention to the heterogeneity of entrepreneurial activities and to the differing motives and aspirations which coexist beneath this common banner. But, following from this, they also yield information about the complex processes of small business activity that is relevant to policy-making. Stanworth and Curran (1981) apply their notion of entrepreneurial 'identities' to the exploration of small business growth potential, which, they suggest, is not merely an automatic 'economic-rational' process, but is as much the outcome of the socially defined meanings which individuals impose upon their proprietorial role (cf Chapter two). Those who assume the 'artisan identity', for instance, may resist growth, even if the business allows it, for fear of undermining those aspects of work (autonomy, control and job-satisfaction) which make proprietorship meaningful and desirable.[4] Alternatively, the four proprietorial 'types' identified by the author are used to point to the differing training and educational needs required to develop small business management (a matter which will be taken up in detail in Chapter seven).

Nevertheless, such typologies are not without their limitations. Apart from the inevitable tendency to oversimplify, there is, certainly in the cases discussed above, a rather limiting concentration upon work-related definitions and meanings and an implicit assumption that 'social identities' are the outcome of social interactions voluntarily entered into by individual actors, shaped by 'negotiation' and experience at the inter-personal level.

Such factors are undeniably important determinants of entrepreneurial career trajectories but they must be set alongside those definitional frameworks which appear external to the individual and provide a moral and ideological 'backdrop' against which inter-personal relations are worked out. Such frameworks will reflect and reproduce wider patterns of inequality and the asymmetric access to power characteristic of capitalist society (Littler and Salaman 1984; Kreckel 1980). One such system of structured inequalities – that of class – has been considered already, but there are two others associated with advanced industrial societies – those of gender and ethnicity (Cockburn 1983; Salaman 1986).

The relationship between gender and small business must be

understood within the wider context of women's situation in industrial society. The dominant ideology and practices of patri- archy have meant that until recently relatively little has been written about the role of women in business and industry which has not been filtered through this distorting lens:

> where they have not been ignored altogether, women in organi- sations have been regarded either as indistinguishable from men in any aspect relevant to their attitudes and actions at work, or as the source of problems for employers and/or the families or communities from which they come.
> (Clegg and Dunkerley 1980:401)

Indeed, until the mid-1980s, recourse to gender as an explanatory variable in small business research had been notable only by its absence (Watson and Watson 1984). Since then, however, interest in female entrepreneurship has intensified, although many of the contributions to this debate are of rather limited analytical poten- tial, being concerned with the specification of differences between samples of male and female entrepreneurs on a number of standard 'business-related' variables (e.g., Solomon and Fernald 1988).

Welsh and Young (1984:15), for instance, conducted a compara- tive analysis of male and female entrepreneurs in the USA with the intention of discovering which dimensions of entrepreneurship have a greater probability of being associated with men or women and which are sex-independent. The dimensions chosen – demo- graphic characteristics, personality traits, perceptions of problems, information source preferences and interest in attending small business seminars – produced profiles of female and male entre- preneurs that were relatively similar, although the typical women entrepreneur emerged as being younger, better educated, more interested in information and more likely to use written informa- tion sources.

In contrast to this rather 'narrow' approach, the principal UK studies of women in business have more often attempted to link the experiences of women entrepreneurs to wider patterns of gender relations. Goffee and Scase (1985) locate their study of fifty-four women small business proprietors within a framework of female subordination arising from the structure of advanced industrial societies. They suggest that

> there are two major ways whereby women individually can tackle their subordination; namely, through the pursuit of careers and through business start-up. Given the concentration

of women in lower-paid, secondary-sector occupations, the opportunities available for personal success through upward mobility within careers are likely to be severely restricted ... the entrepreneurial strategy offers an alternative route for those who wish to escape their conditions of economic and social subordination.

(Goffee and Scase 1985:30–2)

In many respects, this approach has similarities with Stanworth and Curran's (1982) discussion of social marginality, which they define as the perceived incongruity between the individual's personal attributes or self-image and the role he or she holds in society. Entrepreneurship may thus be interpreted as an attempt to maintain a sense of personal autonomy and control in the face of a marginalizing or stigmatizing social role. Although these writers do not themselves include women amongst their examples of the socially marginal, Hertz (1987) has argued that in the predominantly masculine world of conventional business organizations, women form a group with no secure position, often denied access to positions of power and that, as such, it should be expected that they will look for alternative ways to create their own opportunities.

On the basis of their detailed interviews, however, Goffee and Scase (1985:54) conclude that this route to proprietorship is 'highly influenced' by two sets of factors: attachment to entrepreneurial ideals (i.e., a belief in economic self-advancement, individualism, and strong support for the work ethic) and attachment to conventional gender roles, ('the extent to which women accept their subordination to men'). Using these dimensions they construct a typology of female business proprietors, Figure 3.1.

Conventional women business owners, according to Goffee and Scase, are those who start businesses on the basis of 'skills acquired through performing traditional female roles' (e.g., guest

Figure 3.1 Types of female entrepreneur

		Attachment to conventional gender roles	
		High	*Low*
Attachment to entrepreneurial ideals	High	(1) Conventional	(2) Innovative
	Low	(3) Domestic	(4) Radical

Source: Goffee and Scase 1985:55

houses, secretarial and nursing agencies, restaurants, catering firms and hairdressing salons). Such women, because they are highly attached to both entrepreneurial ideals and conventional gender roles, are likely to experience conflicting pressures from their business commitments on the one hand, and their domestic-based personal relationships on the other. This can result in 'a tendency for profit-making to be achieved through strict cost-effectiveness within stable no-growth businesses' (Goffee and Scase 1985:55).

Innovative proprietors, on the other hand, are strongly motivated by profit and business growth and make business ownership a central life interest to which all other personal relationships are subordinate. For these women, 'proprietorship offers them new personal identities. There is a tendency for such women to be unmarried and to have few friends. They have often encountered male prejudices in the labour market' (Goffee and Scase 1985:55). Such women are likely to have been relatively highly educated and to have started careers in large organizations, only to be confronted by 'blocks' to their upward mobility imposed by the so-called 'glass ceiling effect', whereby gender-related characteristics serve as the basis for a lack of recognition and progress beyond relatively junior levels in the organization (Carter and Cannon 1988). The businesses run by such women will be based on technical and professional skills which are developed beyond the constraints imposed by conventional gender roles.

Domestic traders have a low attachment to entrepreneurial ideals but are strongly attached to the traditional female role. As such their businesses take second place to their roles as mothers and wives. Like the conventional proprietors, they tend to trade in a variety of traditional female skills. 'This pattern of trading is characterised by its very small scale nature and by the fact that it is circumscribed by the demands and obligations of the family system' (Goffee and Scase 1985:56).

Radical proprietors, like the innovators, tend to be well qualified and educated, often university graduates, who have suffered similar experiences of gender-based discrimination in large organizations. However, rather than representing an alternative means of career advancement, their businesses offer a means of positive challenge to male domination and prejudices. Their businesses are not geared primarily to profits, and accumulated assets are used to further the longer-term interests of women. Enterprise activity tends to be oriented to the women's movement and can include such diverse operations as publishing, printing, craft trades, retailing, education and small-scale manufacture. In line with the strong egalitarian ethos of the women's movement there is a tendency for ownership to be organized on the basis of jointly owned partnerships and co-operatives.

Given the lack of attention which has been directed towards female entrepreneurship, the Goffee and Scase typology, seeking as it does to locate women business owners within the wider context of socially constructed gender relations as well as purely business variables, represents something of a step foward. Indeed, Cromie and Hayes (1988) and Cromie (1987) have produced data from Northern Ireland which lend (qualified) support to the 'types' identified by Goffee and Scase. Cromie and Hayes, in fact, develop their own typology of female entrepreneurs – 'innovators', 'dualists' and 'returners' – which, whilst differing from Goffee and Scase in certain respects, appears to complement their work rather than contradict it.

One of the confusions to have emerged with these typologies, however (although not necessarily of the authors' own making), is a tendency to treat the 'types' as 'typifications' and to afford them an air of representativeness and generality that the narrowness of the empirical base makes difficult to sustain in any rigorous sense.

To some extent this problem is reduced by the availability of the GHS data-base discussed in the previous chapter (Curran and Burrows 1988) which can serve as a 'bench mark' against which small-scale qualitative research findings can be assessed. Thus, taking the Goffee and Scase data on women entrepreneurs, it seems that only in one area does the GHS data seriously call into question the validity of the typological assumptions, and even here there remains room for argument.

The principal area of contention, according to Curran and Burrows (1988), is that of marital status. In particular they take issue with the view of Goffee and Scase (and others, e.g., Watson and Watson 1984) that for a substantial proportion of women business is a central life interest to the extent that all other personal relationships are secondary, and that business ownership offers women a way to escape economic domination by men and to establish their independence outside the conventional marriage relationship. The basis for Curran and Burrows's query is that the GHS data reveal the proportion of small business proprietors and self-employed who are married (both women and men) to be higher than for the employed population as a whole, whilst the level of divorce or separation for women is markedly lower (for women small business owners 1.6 per cent as against 5.6 per cent for the female employed population). Although they claim not to endorse such an assumption, it seems implicit in Curran and

Burrows's objection that the existence of a marital relationship is indicative of the centrality of that relationship to the women concerned. Clearly it could be argued that to 'establish independence *outside* the conventional marriage relationship' or to subordinate the marriage relationship to business interests, does not necessarily imply the dissolution or absence of that relationship (indeed, this would seem to be a commonplace assumption for male subjects).

On other matters, however, Curran and Burrows's findings on female entrepreneurs are generally supportive of other research in the area. They confirm the three-to-one male–female ratio among small business owners and the self-employed and note that this shows a significant under-representation of women in the small business sector compared to their participation in the economy as employees (which stood at about 44 per cent for the period covered by the survey). Significantly, they point to the fact that whilst the number of women entering small business has increased this has also been true for men, with the relative shares of each sex remaining roughly the same (men having a slightly steeper growth gradient than women [1988:12]).

There are a number of factors which can account for this under-representation. Carter and Cannon (1988) identify a general feeling amongst female entrepreneurs that it is difficult for women to acquire the basic business skills and knowledge which allow entrepreneurship to be approached with confidence. Coupled to this is an awareness of the informal constraints upon women's activity, and expected roles, in the labour market. Both aspects are often absorbed throughout early life and education and reflect the general social patterning of 'conventional' female roles. Overcoming these role expectations may add an additional hurdle to those normally encountered in any business start-up. In addition to such social conditioning, however, Carter and Cannon (1988:570) and Goffee and Scase (1985) both report that their women respondents felt they experienced direct gender-based discrimination, particularly in relation to raising capital for business start-up. Over half of the sample of seventy questioned by Carter and Cannon reported difficulties in raising capital and their respondents generally perceived such difficulties to be gender-related. In particular, bank managers and other lenders were felt to give the impression that they did not see women as credible business proprietors, placing undue emphasis on lack of security and track records. This point is also mentioned by Goffee and Scase, who point to the fact that few of their respondents possessed the necessary financial resources for complete economic independence at the start of trading. Thus, they were either compelled to seek loans from banks (where they reported similar responses to those above) or were forced to have male business partners for the purposes of negotiating credit and for acting as financial guarantors.

Such patterns of direct and indirect discrimination against female entrepreneurs are also relevant to further findings from the GHS data relating to the socio-economic background of women small business proprietors. It seems that slightly over 27 per cent of female small business owners and self-employed, as compared to 16 per cent of all employers, come from employer, managerial or professional family backgrounds. Whereas almost half of all employees came from manual family backgrounds, 37.3 per cent of women in business for themselves did so. Curran and Burrows interpret this as a reflection of the greater difficulties faced by women setting up their own business which needs to be partially offset by the advantages that go with higher socio-economic background, such as greater access to family sources of capital, greater self-confidence and higher levels of educational attainment (Curran and Burrows 1988:30).

These sorts of gender-related difficulties also help to explain the concentration of female-owned businesses in the service sector of the economy: just over 90 per cent of female, compared to 65 per cent of male, small business owners run an enterprise in this sector. Not only is this the bastion of traditional 'female skills' but it is also the sector where the least amount of capital is likely to be required for start-up, since trading can frequently be commenced on the basis of personal skills alone (Scase and Goffee 1982). It is also, of course, an area where (male) lenders may feel that women have the necessary competence to succeed, closely paralleling as it does conventional non-work gender roles.

The research on female entrepreneurs clearly gives some support to the notion that business ownership can represent one means for individuals to combat socially generated and sustained marginal role expectations. What is also clear, however, is that for women this particular route is by no means free from the stigma and discrimination associated with marginality; neither is it equally accessible to all women. In the latter respect it seems that, as in other areas of social life, gender-related disadvantages are reinforced by those associated with socio-economic background.

The notion of social marginality as a stimulus to entrepreneurial activity, whilst clearly applicable to the case of female business owners, has most frequently been applied to the phenomenon of 'ethnic enterprise', particularly that associated with Indian and

Asian communities. The simplest account of such a process is given by Forester: 'Humiliated and discriminated against in the jobs market of white society, their pride injured and qualifications ignored, Asians in Britain have turned to self-employment and entrepreneurial experimentation' (Forester 1978:420).

Jones and McEvoy (1986) provide a more sophisticated explanation which rests upon the notion of a double exclusivity: on the one hand, the tendency of migrant ethnic communities to constitute themselves as an exclusive group vis-à-vis the receiving society; on the other hand, the tendency for the receiving society to exclude migrant groups from full social, political and economic participation (thereby reinforcing the original exclusiveness). Referring to these two processes Jones and McEvoy (1986:199) draw attention to the role of social networks in facilitating small business activity. Ethnic solidarity, they claim, provides a vital business resource, since it represents a potential source of capital, with borrowing and lending based on mutual trust of fellow group members. It also supports customer loyalty, as buyers tend to patronize firms run by their own group members and can even supply cheap labour. As these authors are quick to point out, however, caution is necessary in attaching any measure of importance to these processes. In particular, there has been a tendency for commentators to use this model of the ethnic business formation process (which by definition will be an over-simplification) to support one particularly well-developed stereotype of typical characteristics of an ethnic group, namely that Asians are, by nature, entrepreneurial.

There are now empirical data which question the generality and inevitability of the 'Asian entrepreneur' conventional wisdom. In particular, it challenges the strength of the supposed link between Asian ethnic origin and entrepreneurial ability and the primacy of Asians as the most entrepreneurial of ethnic groups. A study of Asian shopkeepers in Bradford (Aldrich *et al.* 1986), for example, revealed that despite an impressively large absolute number of Asian outlets, this represented self-employment for at most 5 per cent of the city's economically active Asians. This study also revealed that whilst they were more likely to survive longer in business, Asian shopkeepers reported lower profits than whites in the sample; they also worked longer hours. Jones and McEvoy's conclusion is that members of the Asian community, rather than representing a 'fountain of business talent', tend to operate in 'residual niches in the economy abandoned by whites, accepting whatever limited opportunities are available rather than competitively ousting white rivals' (Jones and McEvoy 1986:207).

Similarly, evidence is also now being produced that qualifies the significance attached to 'entrepreneurial networks' of the sort described by Jones and McEvoy. Saker (1989), for example, points out that the support provided by the social network at the time of business formation can, all too quickly, turn into an Achilles heel if the business needs to develop, for although it can increase the propensity for business start-up by reducing the barriers imposed by the institutional framework, it can also lead to potential weaknesses such as the lack of a structured, thought-out business plan. This, in turn, can result in ineffective marketing and a consequent reliance upon the network itself for trade, reinforcing marginality and limiting potential for expansion. The problem is that network-reliant businesses of this sort often tend to be geographically localized: the resources of the network provide all businesses in an area with comparable levels of competitive advantage (e.g., cheap labour and finance) but this is only realized when competing with others outside the network. As a result of the marginality which gave rise to the network, however, such external competition may be severely limited, with the result that network businesses compete mainly against each other, thereby nullifying their competitive advantage and limiting their prospects for wider growth (Saker 1989:9).

Finally, there is the evidence of the GHS, which also provides some illuminating findings on the small business propensities of other ethnic minorities. Some support for the entrepreneurial tendencies of many ethnic minorities is found but, as Curran and Burrows explain, these differences should not be exaggerated:

> popular conceptions of the propensity of non-whites to be in business for themselves or self-employed are supported, but in a limited fashion by the data: in 1979 over 90% of black respondents in the GHS sample of the working population were employees and in 1984, though a higher proportion were working for themselves, over 85% remained employees of somebody else. Put alternatively, on average, for the six years covered, well over 90% of all small business owners in the GHS were white. (Curran and Burrows 1988:42–3)

Additionally, when they separate out the entrepreneurial propensity of different ethnic groups the resulting picture is less than straightforward. Asian men, for example, are almost 50 per cent more likely to run a small business than white British men, but men from Mediterranean and 'European/Rest of the World' backgrounds are *more* likely to own a small business than Asians, whereas Afro-Caribbeans are very under-represented.

Overall, then, the evidence on ethnic involvement in small business would seem to indicate that whilst there may be distinct social processes which push some members of ethnic communities towards this option the extent of this effect should not be exaggerated. Social marginality and entrepreneurial networks may be a spur to entrepreneurship but, as with women business owners, they are not a panacea for widespread discrimination and distrust, neither is small business an automatic or easy option for all in marginal situations. There is, it seems, more than a sprinkling of idealism in the notion that small business can somehow magically solve the problems of those who have otherwise been socially disadvantaged, an idealism which recurs in the study of small business employment relations. Here, it is frequently asserted, the intimacy and personal nature of the small organization offer a healthy and harmonious counter to the alienation and conflicts of interest associated with large-scale capitalist industry. The following chapter sets out to correct this portrayal.

Chapter four

Employment relations in small firms

A great deal of small business research, as the previous chapter revealed, has been concerned with the study of small business owners, their motives, prospects and problems. Although not completely ignored, relatively little attention has been devoted to small business workers. This does not mean, however, that there are not firmly held beliefs about how such workers think, feel and behave. Indeed, a core of such beliefs has come to form what Rainnie has termed a 'conventional wisdom' (Rainnie 1983). In essence, this asserts that the quality of personal relations within small firms – both between employer and workers and between workers themselves – is such as to promote a spirit of co-operation, mutual respect and moral attachment. In short, industrial harmony.

There can be little doubt that this view gained enormously in respectability when it was endorsed by the influential Bolton Report:

> In many respects the small firm provides a better environment for the employee than is possible in most large firms. Although physical working conditions may sometimes be inferior in small firms, most people prefer to work in a small group where communications present fewer problems: the employees in the small firm can easily see the relation between what they are doing and the objectives and performance of the firm as a whole. Where management is more direct and flexible, working rules can be varied to suit the individual . . . . No doubt mainly as a result of this, the turnover of staff in small firms is very low and strikes and other kinds of industrial dispute are relatively infrequent.
> (Bolton 1971:21)

Unfortunately, Bolton's view of the small firm is based upon an extremely limited empirical base. According to Stanworth and

69

Curran (1979) the industrial harmony thesis is founded largely on the uncorroborated opinions of employers, supplemented by a rather narrow reading of a small-scale study of small-firm employees conducted by Ingham (1967; 1970) in the late 1960s.

Ingham was concerned to re-examine the so-called 'size effect' which had emerged as a topic of academic debate in the 1950s and 1960s. This provided a body of research which, through the measurement of labour turnover and absenteeism, purported to show an inverse relationship between size and organizational attachment. In other words, as size decreased so workers became more 'attached' to their employing organization, as manifested by lower rates of absenteeism and labour turnover. Ingham suggested that the low level of bureaucracy associated with small firms created the potential for close personal relationships between employer and employed and between fellow workers and, hence, high levels of attachment. This in itself was nothing new. What was novel about Ingham's work, however, was that it sought to relate the realisation of this potential to the attitudes and aspirations ('orientation to work') held by workers in small firms. Only when there was congruence between the employee's orientation to work and the conditions provided by the small firm would high levels of attachment result. The particular orientation most likely to result in congruence was termed 'non-economistic expressive', in that those holding it could be expected to place a higher value on non-material rewards, such as job satisfaction and pleasant interpersonal relationships, than on purely financial returns. Those holding such an orientation, it was suggested, would thus 'self-select' to work in small firms. Whilst Ingham himself emphasized the contingent nature of this thesis, his work has frequently been wrongly cited as a straightforward confirmation of the propositions (a) that small firms are *inherently* conducive to high levels of employee attachment; and (b) that *all* small-firm workers choose such employment because it offers non-material satisfactions, such as close personal relationships, job satisfaction and involvement, which they value highly. Such an interpretation seems implicit in the Bolton Report, as it does in later statements by those subscribing to the industrial harmony thesis.

Unfortunately, the growth of research findings has done nothing to confirm either the simplicity of the industrial harmony thesis or the generality of Ingham's findings on the attitudes and values of small business workers. The work of Stanworth and Curran is particularly noteworthy in this respect. In a series of articles (e.g., 1978; 1979) reporting the results of a reasonably large study of employment relations in small firms in the printing and electronics industries, they call into question the twin notions that small firms necessarily provide conditions conducive to industrial harmony and that workers self-select such employment because of its ability to yield intrinsic satisfactions. Workers' orientations, they found, were not neatly related to size of firm, nor were they of much importance in explaining the differences between the labour forces of small and large firms. Of more importance were workers' market situations and employers' selection practices, both of which were largely beyond the worker's control. Thus, workers in small firms were younger, less well trained and less experienced than those in large firms, and tended to work in small firms not as the result of 'self selection' but because their lack of training and previous work experience ruled out the possibility of working in large firms (Stanworth and Curran 1978:627–8). Similarly, these writers caution against exaggerating the closeness of employer–employee relations in small firms:

> while friendly social exchanges may take place between owner-managers and employees, shopfloor workers themselves tend to regard these as superficial. They do not fundamentally alter the employer–employee relationship .... When workers were asked about the conditions under which they would go on strike, there was no difference in the proportions of workers in small and large firms who said they would never strike under any circumstances [just 10 per cent].
> (Stanworth and Curran 1978:629)

What emerges clearly from Stanworth and Curran's works is that the differences between workers in large and small firms can easily be overstated. Stanworth and Curran suggest that differences which do emerge are as likely to result from factors external to particular workplaces, such as labour market conditions or industrial subculture (defined as 'the technology and other meanings, definitions and industrial social practices peculiar to an industry') as they are to stem from size alone. In a capitalist economy, they point out, employment relations in small and large firms share the common feature of being based upon the 'cash-nexus': small business workers' relations with their employers are not 'magically rid of the contradictions of interest and outlook which inevitably surround economic activities in capitalist society' (Stanworth and Curran 1979:337).

Stanworth and Curran provide a body of thorough empirical work which casts doubt upon the industrial harmony thesis as a general explanation of small business employment relations. In effect, however, their research only partially undermines these arguments: it shows that industrial harmony is not a consequence of individual employee attitudes (since these appear to differ little between employees in small and large firms), that workers in small firms face the same economic constraints as their large business counterparts, and that they do not necessarily seem any more attached to their employers. What it does less adequately is to explain why employment in small firms elicits *behaviour* (as opposed to *attitudes*) from workers that gives the appearance of industrial harmony. The fact remains that small firms *do* experience less industrial action and lower rates of trade union- ism than larger firms. A rough indication for manufacturing industries is given in Table 4.1. In the service sector (for which comparable figures are not available) it is likely that both union membership and incidence of industrial action are lower (Pearson 1985).

Table 4.1 Union representation and industrial action by size of establishment

Proportion of establishments that recognized manual unions in relation to independence (%) (private sector only)

	Total	1–24	25–49	50–99	100–99	200+
All establishments	50	25	43	63	78	91
Independent establishments	31	16	24	50	66	67
Establishments that were part of a group	58	28	55	68	81	92

Establishments experiencing any type of industrial action – by number of manual workers

Size	1–9	10–24	25–49	50–99	100–99	200–499	500–999	1000+
Percentage experiencing any form of industrial action	2	8	13	27	33	50	74	77

Source: Rainnie 1989:28

To arrive at an adequate explanation of this apparent paradox, it is necessary to shift the analysis away from the attitudes of those involved and towards the constraints associated with the employ- ment relationship. The central theoretical tool of such investiga- tion is the concept of 'control' (Scott and Rainnie 1982:47ff). Employers, be they of large or small firms, do not merely buy the labour of their workers, they have to ensure that such labour is controlled – i.e., exercised in such a way as to make the operation of the enterprise viable in the market. There is, however, no guarantee that workers will accept such control willingly or without resistance or, alternatively, adapt its exercise to suit their own interests. The manner in which employers are able to exercise control, therefore, depends upon a number of factors which affect the relative balance of power between the parties. Thus, although control of the employment relationship is a necessary condition for the operation of any business, the precise way in which such control is exercised is subject to wide variation (Wood 1982; Littler and Salaman 1982).

In the case of small firms specifically, the key to understanding the exercise of control lies in two related concepts: the dependence of the employer upon particular employees and vice versa; and the power of workers individually or collectively to resist the exercise of proprietorial prerogative. Where employers are heavily dependent upon employees, for example, workers may experience little need to resist the exercise of proprietorial prerogative: employers, consciously or unconsciously, in an attempt to maintain the commitment of their employees and hence make the management of dependence reliable, adopt modes of control felt to be congruent with the expectations of their employees. Using these two dimensions it is possible to describe four types of small-firm employer control strategy as shown in the typology, Figure 4.1. These will be examined in turn below.

Figure 4.1 Types of employer control in small firms

	High		
Extent of		1. Fraternalism	
employer's		2. Paternalism	
economic			3. Benevolent
dependence			Autocracy
upon employees			4. Sweating
	Low		

	High		Low
		Ability of employees to	
		resist the exercise	
		of proprietorial prerogative	

1 Fraternalism

This strategy (which has been elaborated in detail through the work of Scase and Goffee 1982; Goffee and Scase 1982) reflects a high level of employer dependence upon workers who provide labour that is both vital to the success of the business and in short supply in the labour market. As described by Scase and Goffee fraternalism gives all the appearances not only of industrial harmony but also of egalitarianism. Employers work alongside their employees and frequently pay themselves a wage at the same rate (benefiting from their proprietorial position through end-of-year profits and fiscal perks), claiming that this makes the employment relationship one between fellow work-mates rather than boss and worker; the employer 'earns his keep' rather than merely living off the labour of others. The strategy is not simply about being fair to employees or salving the employer's conscience, however. It is also, and perhaps primarily, a means of 'handling' workers whose skills are both essential to the business and in short supply.

> The dependence of small employers on their workers is heightened by the fact that they typically employ only [a small number of employees] .... Consequently, the poor performance – or absence – of one [worker] can have a disproportionately large impact on productivity. This vulnerability emphasises small employers' reliance on their [employees] working together as equals in a team which 'pulls together'. If this all-round effort is not achieved the consequences can be disastrous.
> (Goffee and Scase 1982:115)

A crucial part of this strategy, therefore, is the employer's respect for that occupational 'custom and practice' which is felt to be valued by employees. In the case of the building trade described by Scase and Goffee, this includes the belief that close supervision of skilled employees transgresses traditional norms of craft autonomy and shows a lack of trust in the skills and self-direction of the workers. In such circumstances, direct supervisory control or surveillance can result in poor performance or open defiance, as the following quotation from one of their respondents illustrates: 'If I call at the job too many times then they obviously get the idea that I'm checking up on them ... then they have two hours for lunch' (Scase and Goffee 1982:111). A further extension of fraternalism is the provision of fringe benefits, such as small loans or the use of plant and materials for jobs 'on the side' (see Chapter three).

Later work by Goffee and Scase on women entrepreneurs describes a similar strategy of control utilized by 'innovative' proprietors (see Chapter three) which they label 'egalitarianism' (Goffee and Scase 1985:65ff). Here also the emphasis is upon the control of 'key' workers in a manner which both sustains commitment and stabilises economic dependence upon their services, primarily through the granting of considerable degrees of autonomy and discretion within work tasks. This approach parallels the patterns of employment relations frequently associated with 'professional' small businesses and those in high-technology industries. In the professions, for instance, the loyalty and commitment of key workers are often maintained through the offering of partnerships in the business, usually dependent upon satisfactory performance and service, although a capital sum may also be required (i.e., to 'buy in' to the practice). Indeed, the whole tenor of professional education is to create the expectation that creative work demands high levels of discretion and trust, and that employer and employee will relate to each other as colleagues rather than superior and subordinate (Fox 1974). Thus, to provide such conditions is not only likely to be part of the 'culture' of a profession but also the only way in which a practitioner can retain the services of other, albeit less well-established, professionals.

Similar concerns operate in areas of new technology where highly qualified and innovative scientific workers are in short supply. For such professional workers, therefore, small businesses offer what Handy refers to as a 'Person Culture':

Control mechanisms, or even management hierarchies, are impossible in these cultures except by mutual consent. The psychological contract states that the organization is subordinate to the individual and depends on the individual for its existence. The individual can leave the organization but the organization seldom has the power to evict the individual. Influence is shared and the power base, if needed, is usually expert; that is, individuals do what they are good at and are listened to on appropriate topics.
(Handy 1978:195–6)

Additionally, in some high-technology firms, it seems, not only does the organization have to develop a culture congruent with the expectations of 'scarce' creative workers, but it may also have to provide a wider 'environmental package' attractive to such employees e.g., by being located in areas of 'high-quality' residential and cultural provision (Keeble and Kelly 1986; Chapter six of this book). This rosy picture of employment relations in high-technology small business does require qualification in that the extension of such favourable terms and conditions is very much restricted to 'central' creative workers. For many lesser skilled employees involved in routine production or servicing tasks, conditions and treatment are frequently very different, often involving short-term contracts, sudden redundancy, and relatively poor wages.

The point remains, therefore, that fraternalism and related strategies such as egalitarianism are not merely the result of an empathy between employer and employed – industrial harmony pure and simple. They are sustained in no small measure by prevailing economic conditions: namely, a tight labour market for key workers, who expect to be afforded a high degree of trust and discretion in the exercise of their skills and whose commitment is vital to the success of the business.

Under other conditions fraternalism would prove an inappropriate means of control. Where, for example, skilled work is not a requirement and competent workers are readily available, it can appear to employers an expensive and unnecessary 'luxury'. Alternatively, where diligent, skilled and loyal workers are required but where the socio-economic 'gap' between employer and employees is great (and/or labour market pressure less acute), attempts to foster fraternalism are likely to face suspicion (or derision) from workers. It is precisely these circumstances that Newby (1977) associates with an alternative small employer strategy, that of 'paternalism'.

2 Paternalism

Paternalism, then, arises in situations where the employer's dependence upon labour is less pressing, although not unimportant, and where the position of workers is such as to limit their power to resist proprietorial prerogative. Unlike fraternalism, which seeks to organize workers without recourse to clearly defined hierarchical control, the differentiation of employer and employed is at the centre of paternalism. At the same time, however, this strategy also seeks to foster the apparently contradictory objective of cultivating the identification of subordinates with their 'superiors'. In the case of agriculture, where Newby's (1977) account provides the most complete examination, this paradox is a reflection of both the work situation on small farms and the traditional status of landowners in rural communities. The striking difference in material wealth and social status between the property-owning farmer and the poorly paid farm labourer dependent upon tied housing cannot easily be disguised by fraternalist strategies, which would be 'unrealistic' in practical terms and undermine the traditional social relationships of rural life. In farming in particular, where the avenues of mobility from farm worker to landowning (or even renting) proprietor are severely restricted and where family inheritance provides the principal route of access to agricultural capital, the pattern of class relations has a great degree of stability: 'Successive generations of agricultural workers are confronted with a reality which becomes to them self-evident. There have always been bosses and workers, farmers and farm workers, master and man – and there always will be' (Newby 1977:369). This, of course, is in stark contrast to an industry such as building, where the route between employee and self-employed or small employer is well trodden and accessible. In this aspect of the employment relationship, then, farm workers appear relatively powerless. But against this must be set their role in the modern agricultural labour process which demands not only high levels of skill but also the ability to work unsupervised and to be in direct control of their employer's valuable assets (often land, livestock and machinery). In this respect the employer is again heavily dependent upon the good services of the employee, over and above the minimal demands of the cold cash-nexus, hence the need to encourage workers' identification with the employer's goals.

The strategy of paternalism seeks to secure this by using the close personal nature of the employment relationship to establish bonds of *mutual* duty and obligation which extend beyond the narrow sphere of work and which are intended to demonstrate that existing inequalities are, in fact, beneficial to subordinates as well as their superiors. Paternalism, thus, requires employers to possess the 'wherewithal' to sustain their claim to legitimate traditional authority, usually by the application of some substantive and/or symbolic form of reinforcement involving duties beyond the wage contract – typically 'gifts' of one form or another that are expected to evoke feelings of gratitude and affection among employees (Newby 1977:429). These 'gifts' go beyond the small loans provided by fraternal employers and may extend not only to the provision of housing but also to the sympathetic exercise of influence in the local community (e.g., local or parish councils, etc.). The effect of this 'amorphous web' of personally conducted patenalistic relations is described by Newby thus:

[Paternalism] renders the industrial relations of agriculture extremely resistant to outside influence .... Whatever the appallingly low wages that are prevalent in agriculture, how can the individual employer, who is such a kind and considerate person, be held responsible for such exploitation? This is *not* a case of the wicked squire grinding the faces of the poor into the earth .... Farmers *individually* do not represent the

'unacceptable face of capitalism', but capitalism at its most considerate and socially responsible .... Paternalism therefore has the consequence of wrong-footing the agricultural worker ... they find it difficult given the nature of their relationship with the farmer to blame him for their poverty.
(Newby 1977:431)

For paternalistic control to be effective, therefore, it is necessary for there to be a significant level of 'isolation' surrounding the employment relationship. That is to say, employees' access to alternative definitions of that relationship must be restricted. Thus paternalism is likely to be most effective where workplaces are small (i.e., the particularistic relations between employer and employee are not cross-cut by 'alternative' attachments to work groups or trade unions), and/or localized, thereby restricting access to alternative types of employment and, hence, alternative meaning systems.

Clearly paternalism is not as adaptable as fraternalism, its application being restricted to a limited range of employment situations. Similarly, the articulation of dependence and resistance is more complex: employers are indeed dependent upon workers to a considerable extent for the economic success of their enterprise but, simultaneously, paternalism is only viable where workers are also heavily dependent upon an individual employer for jobs. Under these conditions workers may appear to endorse the moral authority of the employer – and even to benefit from it – but this harmony, frequently attributed to personalized employer–employee interactions, is in practice as much the outcome of a complex economic relationship reflecting the distribution of socio-economic power as personal preference. Newby makes clear that the apparently deferential behaviour of farm workers towards their paternalistic employers does not necessarily signal moral endorsement, or even contentment with their lot, but rather a pragmatic realization that their situation is such as to make open resistance a less attractive proposition than compliance. In other words, workers realize that they have a better chance of improving their position by 'playing along' with their employer than by, say, engaging in conventional industrial action such as strikes, etc.

The diffuse social obligations and duties upon which paternalism is founded, however, are not entirely within the control of the employer. Changes in market forces may mean that the obligations traditionally expected from a paternalistic employer become increasingly difficult to meet. Such events as redundancies, evictions from tied housing, or deskilling, can make paternalism unworkable by imposing the impersonal logic of the market upon what was formerly defined as a diffuse social relationship. Such redefinition is likely to be perceived by workers as a betrayal or breach of trust, making the reestablishment of paternalism unviable and recasting the employment relationship in more conventional conflictual terms (Martin and Fryer 1973; Lane and Roberts 1971). In its rigorous form, therefore, paternalism is not a 'simple' or 'easy' control strategy for small employers to adopt. Indeed, its very success is premised upon the possession of sufficient time and resources to devote to the obligations and duties involved. In practice it is likely to remain a declining form of control, even in its last stronghold of agriculture.

Although they have attracted a good deal of attention, neither fraternalism nor paternalism could claim to be typical of small business managerial strategies. More commonly described, but less frequently analysed, is an approach which can be labelled 'benevolent autocracy'.

3 Benevolent autocracy

Here the articulation of dependency and resistance is less clear-cut. A more limited dependence upon employees allows employers to stamp the employment relationship with their personal authority, but this is a function simply of their positional power (i.e., as an employer) rather than the result of an elaborate web of paternalistic relations. On the other hand, employees are neither so independent as to warrant (or be able to demand) fraternal treatment, nor so dependent as to be susceptible to crude economic coercion.

Benevolent autocracy emphasizes the 'closeness' of the links between employer and employee but does not seek to cultivate the employment relationship in directions which extend beyond the workplace or which lead to expectations of employer obligations towards employees that override the exigencies of the market. This type of employment relationship thus combines in a vital tension cordial and particularistic employer–employee interactions with the impersonal dictates of market forces; it attempts to handle conflicts of economic interest and outlook within a context which depends upon both parties at least 'getting along' together at a personal level.[1] Because of this tension benevolent autocracy illustrates particularly clearly the way in which conflict can be handled within small firms. In particular, the fragility of the small business employment relationship demands the 'neutralization' of potential conflicts before they become explicit, a fact which bears upon the problem posed by the appearance of industrial harmony alongside the absence of employees' unequivocal moral endorsement of employer objectives.

The author's own research provides concrete examples of the operation of benevolent autocracy and its role in limiting the expression of open conflict in small business employment relations. The data are taken from the instant print sector of the British general printing industry and cover six independent firms employing between one and six workers. Whilst the results cannot be claimed to be statistically representative of either that sector or the industry in general, they nevertheless provide a detailed qualitative picture of the processes involved.[2]

Instant printing is an area of the printing trade which has expanded rapidly in the 1980s, primarily as a function of developments in printing technology which have allowed the production of low- to medium-quality print on a small scale using relatively simple and quick techniques. Coupled to this has been a marketing offensive by a small number of large franchise operations (see Chapter five) that has both widened the services provided by the small printer and made these more accessible to the general public (by the use of prominent high-street shops and advertising campaigns). In the wake of this high-profile campaign a large number of 'independent' instant print shops have also emerged, either new start-ups or 'conversions' from already established small jobbing printers (Goss 1986; 1987).

Unlike traditional methods of printing, the techniques of instant print have been developed to be within the operational capabilities of workers without previous experience or lengthy training in typography or press work. Indeed, it was the ability of employers to make use of cheap labour (compared to rates paid in unionized print shops) that made many of the instant print shops viable businesses. In those firms studied employers showed a marked preference for workers possessing precisely this quality (i.e., 'cheapness'), it being associated with the young and unskilled. Of the eighteen workers employed in the six firms, none were over 30 years of age and 60 per cent were under 20; many were in their first full-time job and over 50 per cent had been unemployed before their present post. It was not only low pay, however, that made young people relatively attractive to small employers. They were also regarded as particularly suitable because of greater flexibility and adaptability to the restricted nature of the work.

In the instant print shops of the study these three factors – low pay, flexibility and undemanding jobs – were closely interrelated. Because of the small size of the firms (the largest employed six persons) even the most unskilled operations if not performed with application and diligence could result in significant losses in productivity. Consequently employers were concerned that workers should be capable of being trained to meet the particular needs of the organization rather than absorbing a specific craft. Similarly, they did not want employees to specialize in a single job, but to move between tasks, taking the role of 'general hand'. In their experience, restriction to general duties rather than the practice of a specific craft or skill was less acceptable to older more experienced print workers. Finally, there was the important consideration of cost. Not only were younger workers likely to be less 'set in their ways' and more flexible than older workers, they were also more likely to accept what the employer defined as a 'realistic' wage, which meant, in reality, considerably less than would have to be offered to secure the services of a skilled craft worker. The limited experience and lack of formal qualifications and skills meant that the young workers, particularly at a time of high general unemployment, possessed a relatively low estimation of their 'worth' and, given the lack of alternative employment opportunities, were prepared to take what was offered. Small employers were not in the least reticent about driving home their advantage in the labour market by offering terms and conditions on a 'take it or leave it basis', the following quotation being typical of the views expressed: 'I say [to an employee], "Right, I can afford this, is that enough?" He's then got to make the decision, yes it is enough and he will stay, or no it isn't enough and go.'

Unlike fraternal employers having to deal with experienced skilled workers with definite expectations of 'proper' treatment and a strong labour market position, the instant print proprietors had little need to try to conceal the hierarchical nature of the employment relationship from their workers. The imbalance of power between them was sufficiently great effectively to remove the issue of control from the arena of negotiation. In fact, the unconditional authority of the employer was presented as a pre-given and unalterable 'fact' of working life. Thus, rather than define the employment relationship according to notions of traditional paternalism, or on the basis of a shared identity as fellow productive workers, these employers viewed it as reducible to the logic of the market. As they saw it they were paying the piper and therefore had the right to call the tune.

This autocratic dimension, however, forged in the impersonal rationality of the marketplace, was also overlaid by strands of particularism fostered by high levels of face-to-face interaction. Certainly the small employers had to control their employees, to fix their levels of remuneration, to dictate the tasks they were to perform and direct their performance, but they had also to 'get on' with them in the course of everyday work. Not only could bad personal relations make for disgruntled or disloyal workers whose poor performance might imperil productivity; they could also make the daily conduct of working life unpleasant and stressful. In this respect even a relationship based on the employer's exercise of autocratic control needed to embody some element of the 'social' in addition to the purely 'economic'. For the small employers this was achieved by treating employees consciously as individuals, encouraging the use of first names, the sharing of conversations and jokes. The effect was to imprint the impersonal economic power available to the employer with the stamp of personal, even charismatic, authority. Unlike the 'person culture' associated with fraternalism, benevolent autocracy is closely tied to a 'power culture':

> If this culture had a patron god it would be Zeus, the all-powerful head of the Gods of Ancient Greece who ruled by whim and by impulse, by the thunderbolt and the shower of gold from Mount Olympus. This culture depends on a central power source with rays of power and influence spreading out from the central figure .... Resource power is the major power-base in this culture with some elements of personal power in the centre.
> (Handy 1978:189)

Similarly, unlike the traditional authority of paternalism, the small employers seldom sought to extend their influence to form diffuse or unconditional bonds of friendship beyond the working relationship; the element of differentiation between employer and employed was never completely submerged, but neither did it need elaborate justification.

How, then, did employees respond to this regime? On the face of it, the responses of the young workers appeared to endorse the industrial harmony thesis. Most regarded their boss as a 'nice chap' and spoke of friendly relations within the workplace in a manner suggestive of a high level of employee commitment, even deference. But care must be taken not to remove such endorsements from their particular context. They were not, after all, simply statements of individual attitudes or beliefs, but responses to specific social situations and, as such, reflected the constraints and inequalities of power within the workplace. Thus, although these young workers appeared to acquiesce in their objectively subordinate position, they were not unaware of the material constraints which underpinned this particular balance of power and, in many ways, their acquiescence reflected fear of economic sanctions (which might be imposed by either their employer or, for those on government training schemes, the state). In other words, they were well aware of their tenuous position vis-à-vis the continuation of, or alternative to, their present employment and appeared keen to ensure that this was not jeopardized by any behaviour on their part which might be deemed inappropriate by their employers. The following quotation captures this sense of powerlessness and the way in which personal relations with a superior may, despite the appearance of cordiality, contribute to this:

> You've got to play it by ear and be a bit careful what you say. If the boss starts going on about something, even if you don't agree, you've got to keep quiet and nod your head and pretend to agree, even if you don't. That way you don't get into an argument, you've just got to grin and bear it, humour them almost. You can't want to upset him because you just get picked on, taking the piss and that, until you blow up, and then you're out.

The young workers were particularly aware of their vulnerability in the labour market and guided their behaviour accordingly. But there was also a real sense in which they were ignorant of their situation (a consequence of their age and lack of previous experience) and, in large measure, dependent upon the definitions of the work situation provided by their employers (and/or the government training scheme).[3] Thus, not only did they lack previous work experience with which they could compare, and hence assess, their present position, they were also confined to a work situation where their employers effectively could restrict access to meaning systems or definitions deemed 'inappropriate'. In general there were no older workers or trade union officials from whom they might receive an alternative view of the employment relationship. Indeed, on the issue of trade unionism not only were these small business workers unclear as to the role or utility of union membership but, in most cases, they were totally ignorant as to which unions were active in the printing industry. There can be little doubt that in this area the ignorance of these young workers was compounded, if not actively encouraged, by the strong anti-union stance of their employers. Certainly within the context of the workplace these young workers were both ideologically and economically subordinated to their employers. Not only did most of them appear to lack the articulateness and self-confidence that would have enabled them to challenge, or even question, the definitions offered by the self-assured and highly opinionated small employers, but any attempt at resistance could be potentially dangerous to their position: as the quotations above indicate, dissent is not to be taken lightly within the context of small business employment relations.

The case of instant printing represents a clear example of the ways in which the superior economic and ideological power of small business employers can be exercised within the context of personalized and particularistic employment relations to create the appearance of industrial harmony. In this case the principal mechanism facilitating the small employers' control over their workers was the operation of the labour market, which enabled the recruitment of those deemed to be compliant, trustworthy, but also relatively powerless. Thus, where conditions allow, benevolent autocracy represents a strategy which is easily accessible to small employers in situations where the normative approval of employees beyond the simple necessity for stable and amicable working relationships is not a significant issue. Directly or indirectly, it is the employer's definition which is imposed upon the employment relationship, albeit within a framework which makes limited accommodative gestures to the 'interests' of employees.

4 Sweating

There are, of course, circumstances in which even these conditional concessions to employees are deemed unnecessary by employers as workers can be recruited and replaced readily without disrupting business activities. Here the principal factor in the employment relationship is cost rather than stability or trustworthiness, a situation facilitated by an employer's minimal level of dependence upon the availability of suitable workers. Employee resistance to control under such circumstances is difficult, either because dismissal and replacement are viable employer options, or because workers themselves are in a dependent position with no source of alternative employment, making passive acquiescence the only possible course of action. In extreme cases such a situation supports the 'sweating' or 'hyper-exploitation' of labour.

The continued existence of sweat-shops provides the most direct challenge to the industrial harmony thesis. These survive in marginal market niches where extreme flexibility of output is a condition of existence. There is no consistent definition of what constitutes a sweat-shop but Hoel provides a useful starting point:

These factories are on the whole small, and the rent paid for the premises is low due to the condition and situation. Basically though ... sweating is related to the arbitrary nature of demand, liability to rush orders and sudden gluts of production which provide manufacturers with no incentive to stockpile. Low wages, low rent and above all reliance on vulnerable female labour, especially that of immigrants, reduces overheads and permits manufacturers to hire and fire at any sign of expansion or contraction of business.
(Hoel 1982:80)

As Hoel makes clear, a weak and vulnerable workforce appears an essential precondition for successful sweating and, in this respect, women from ethnic minorities would seem to be particularly disadvantaged, since racial characteristics may reinforce a sexually determined secondary labour market position. Pearson, for example, explains the situation faced by many such women looking for work and the resulting industrial relations practices of many small firms:

Many small entrepreneurs who set up in the clothing industry are from the same community as their employees .... Community ties do not prevent exploitation .... [As an employee of one such firm reported:] 'Our factory makes over 3,000 dresses a week. But there are only eight of us. We have to tidy up and sweep up on a Friday, and if it is half-past-five and we have not finished, he won't pay us. If we are busy and he wants us in on Saturday, he says, "If you're not coming in Saturday, you are not coming in Monday."'
(Pearson 1985:36)

Hoel describes a similar situation in a small business run by members of the Indian community and employing mainly married women from the Punjab: 'the workers were closely supervised, often working with a supervisor standing behind the rows of machinists ordering them to speed up their work, to shut their mouths and not to move from their seats until lunchtime' (Hoel 1982:83). Under these conditions there is virtually no necessity for employers to attempt to conceal conflict, since direct coercion or, failing this, replacement, are both unproblematic and uncontested. As Levidow remarked of the notorious Grunwick case,

The firm enforced its rules with the threat of sacking, quite freely used for relatively minor infringements .... The management displayed a literally casual attitude towards its workforce in a way that would horrify more enlightened capitalists concerned with exploiting skills more effectively .... The atmosphere suggested by the high turnover of staff in the mail-order department is one in which the development of a settled, long-serving labour force was apparently not a high priority. (Levidow 1981:139)

Concluding the discussion of modes of employer control it can be noted that the typology reveals the complexity and diversity of employment relations in small businesses, these ranging from the egalitarian ethos of *'primus inter pares'* associated with fraternalism to the ruthless exploitation of workers under sweat-shop conditions. Even so, this typology is by no means exhaustive, and as more data become available it is certain that different strategies of control will be identified and existing ones modified or refined. One point which does emerge with some certainty, however, is that there is likely to be only limited support for any simple understanding of small business employment relations as necessarily and essentially harmonious.

Of the relatively few studies which concentrate specifically on small business industrial relations, few have given unequivocal support to the industrial harmony thesis (e.g., Stanworth and Curran 1981; Rainnie 1983; 1984; 1989; Goss 1986; 1988; Stephenson 1983). Westrip, for example, has shown that small firms do, and should be expected to, exhibit a greater tendency to unfairly dismiss workers (Westrip 1982), and Stevens confirms that 'the typical unfair dismissal applicant [will] be a male, manual worker, not in membership of a union, who has been dismissed after relatively short service *by a small employer* in the private sector' (Stevens 1988:659; emphasis added). Similarly, Stanworth and Curran (1979) have demonstrated that small firms are likely to have a higher labour turnover than their larger equivalents. Most recently, Rainnie (1989) has published case-studies of small business industrial relations in the printing and clothing industries which demonstrate that both the nature of employment relations at organizational level, and the structuring of the capitalist economy generally, serve to limit the opportunities for small business workers to engage in explicitly conflictual disputes without severely jeopardizing their position in the labour market. Such evidence, far from supporting the industrial harmony thesis, suggests that conflict is common to small firms but that it tends to be manifested at an individual level (i.e., workers will tend to leave or be dismissed rather than be involved in conventional industrial action) or to be 'neutralized' before it develops to the point of open expression, as illustrated through the previous discussion of benevolent autocracy.

To ignore this evidence and interpret the absence of conventional industrial action as proof of industrial harmony is clearly to offer a grossly simplistic understanding of the nature and effectivity of industrial conflict (Edwards and Scullion 1983). The principal source of confusion in this respect seems to be what Newby has termed 'the easy elision between "interaction with" and "identification with"' (Newby 1977:62), that is to say, the assumption that the close proximity of employer and employed will necessarily lead to harmonious relations and a sense of common purpose. Newby demonstrates the fallacy of this convenient assumption through his study of agricultural workers on small farms, arguing that their quiescent behaviour in the presence of their employers could be understood not as a manifestation of subjective deference but, rather, as a pragmatic response to the economic and ideological powerlessness engendered by the rural class structure. Thus, according to Newby, 'the agricultural worker has acknowledged his powerlessness and decided to make the best of his inferior situation, contriving to take it somewhat for granted whilst not necessarily endorsing it in terms of social justice' (Newby 1977:414). In other words, the mere appearance of compliant, acquiescent behaviour on the part of workers is not sufficient grounds for concluding that this is evidence of commitment to, and identification with, the goals and objectives of the employer and organization.

The operation of similar processes can be illustrated by further examples from the author's research in the printing industry, this time in the field of high-quality colour printing. Here, unlike instant printing, skilled labour remained a necessity and the printing unions had retained control of the labour market; all the firms studied[4] operated 'closed shop' agreements with the National Graphical Association (NGA), the industry's craft union. But these employers were in little doubt that neither the unionization of their workforces nor the formal policies and regulations negotiated with the NGA represented any significant threat to their authority. As one explained,

> The smaller printer like myself can generally get away with murder because we've got a good understanding with our staff. I can talk to them and we can probably come to a good arrangement, but in a large company everything is done by the union rule-book.

87

The owner-managers attributed much of their success in achieving co-operation and harmony to a sense of empathy arising from small-scale organization but, in the course of investigation it became apparent that other factors were also at work. These were factors deriving from the economic base of the enterprise, in particular the ability of employers to manipulate the wage relation, and to play upon the fear of enterprise closure. To understand how such processes operate it is necessary first to describe the formal framework of industrial relations within which these small printing firms operated.

In the organized sectors of the general printing industry the NGA negotiated a national minimum wage for its members which served as the basis for the negotiation of 'house rates' at a domestic level. The size and complexity of such 'house agreements' could be subject to wide variation between companies but with additional benefits tending to be more favourable in larger firms. In small firms chapels tended to be relatively weak, and overtime or bonus payments, which contribute to 'topping up' the minimum wage, less reliable.

The owner-managers in the present study, for instance, paid a basic wage on, or slightly above, the union minimum and 'topped up' only with small bonuses and occasional overtime. Even these, however, were given in such a way as to make clear that their continuity was contingent upon workers' acceptance of flexible working practices. Bonuses, for example, were attached only to individual jobs as and when delivery deadlines made this necessary, rather than being a regular feature of the wage. For workers such conditions meant that many union rules, particularly those relating to demarcation between different craft 'jobs', had to be ignored. It was clearly understood by workers that to insist upon the observance of such rules would jeopardize not only a much-needed bonus but, also, the 'goodwill' of their employer. For despite the existence of the minimum wage, employers retained considerable scope to penalize 'bad' and reward 'good' employees according to their discretion. As one employer explained,

> The union rate is basically used by most firms as a basic rate, as something to guide us; and if we got someone who is good we tend to pay them a little bit more, but if we get someone who just does their job then we give them the bare rate. I think that's the way most people work it.

Indeed, given the relatively low level of the basic wage, the chance of any increased earnings was of considerable importance to the workers. The element of arbitrariness which employers could introduce into this system ensured that such bonuses could not be taken for granted, as might be the case in a larger firm, but remained within the personal prerogative of the employer. The following quotation illustrates the ways in which workers experienced such pressures:

> Like in this firm if you upset them [the bosses] they make it impossible for you to stay. That's the thing with small firms, it's at a personal level. If the bosses don't like you – no matter how good ... you are – you can't stay, it's just miserable.

Amongst employees there was, thus, a clear recognition of conflicting interests between themselves and their employers, even though this was seldom articulated explicitly. Nevertheless, and contrary to views (like those expressed in the Bolton Report) emphasizing the value workers place upon a close relationship with their employers, such 'closeness' was often seen as a distinct problem by those workers in the study. For example,

> When we originally started the boss did work out here doing odd-jobs, but there's nothing worse than the person you actually work for working alongside you. It's alright for a little while, you know, but you're not at ease, you could never be at ease because you would always be tense. You're basically being watched, you could never relax. Nobody obviously does eight hours solid work, it's impossible. You would be so nervous you couldn't do the job.

Such hostility to employer intervention could be explained by the traditions of craft unionism common in the printing trade but, despite the reputation of the printing chapel as 'the most highly developed form of trade union workshop organisation' (Sykes 1967), its real, as opposed to formal, power within these small firms was questionable. In the present study all the firms had a recognized chapel for craft workers but their role was often perceived as less than significant. The conventional notion of the chapel as a vehicle for confrontational and explicitly conflictual industrial relations seemed inappropriate within these small firms. The workers were aware that their employers were unable, or unwilling, to conform with union rules, which restricted the flexibility of labour, and recognized that if they were to safeguard their own positions they could not realistically rely upon the coercive collective power of the union. As one worker cogently remarked,

> It's alright for these newspaper places to keep going out on strike to get what they want, because they've got the muscle to

> do it. If they stop work for a day then everybody knows about it
> because nobody gets a paper; but somewhere like this, no
> bugger's even going to know we're here; it's no difference to
> anyone if a few brochures are a few days late.

For pragmatic reasons, therefore, it was more advantageous for
these small business workers to 'go along' with their employer in
the contravention of formal union regulations (e.g., governing
demarcation between skills and craft and non-craft work) than to
try to prevent this by recourse to conventional conflictual forms of
industrial action or collective coercion. It was not that they were
opposed to the principle of strong trade unionism, but rather that
they were acutely aware of its limitations within the small-scale
workplace. Their main criticisms of their own union were of a
practical nature, namely, that it did not seem well adapted to deal
with the sorts of problems faced by workers in small firms: 'They
cannot call us out on strike without us really thinking about it. If
we went on strike this place would close and that would be the end
of it, my job as well.' In other words, there was the recognition
that within the small firm it was all-but impossible for union
regulation to override the personal authority of the employer at
the practical level. For the owner-manager always held the trump
card: the power to define workers' non-compliance as a potential
contribution to uncompetitiveness, business failure and, of course,
job loss. For these workers, then, the union offered a certain
amount of protection, primarily in terms of minimum wages, but
other potential benefits of collective organization had to be
tempered pragmatically to meet the requirements of small business organization. As one worker explained,

> If [we] carried out every rule in the union hand-book, this place
> ... could not run .... The union doesn't like small shops
> because we do too much, we allow ourselves to be manipulated
> [by our employer], we're not strong enough; and it is a battle, I
> will admit it.

Thus, despite the fact that these workers occupied a relatively
strong labour market position – to the extent that small employers
specializing in this type of printing were dependent upon union
members and accepted this fact through formal agreement with
the NGA – the extent of their ability to turn this into an intra-
organizational bargaining advantage was severely limited. This
limitation was due in no small part to the ability of employers to
emphasize – often accurately – the relative instability of the
enterprises' product market position and the adverse effect which

a non-compliant workforce would have upon jobs, particularly since the definition of what constituted poor performance, both of the organization and the individual worker, remained largely the personal prerogative of the employer.

The above analysis exposes the limitations of an uncritical acceptance of the notion of small business industrial harmony. The arguments and evidence presented indicate that the articulation of conflict and co-operation within small firms may be considerably more complex and contradictory than has frequently been asserted. There is certainly very little reason to retain the notion that there exists a simple correspondence between the formal designation of a business as 'small' and the substantive social relations which constitute it in practice. Indeed, it can be suggested that such formal categorizations of small business are unduly restrictive in areas other than those of employment relations. In particular, they implicitly concentrate attention only upon private independently owned enterprises with a 'legitimate' legal form. This, however, ignores other forms of economic activity which could, arguably, be included under the broad heading of small business. These 'alternative' forms of small business and their associated social relations are discussed in the following chapter.

Chapter five

Alternative forms of small business

It has long been recognized that not all work, even paid work, takes place in the 'formal' economy. In the late 1970s and early 1980s this notion had attracted the interest of sociologists, resulting in numerous attempts to delineate the boundaries of the different 'economies' operating in any given society (e.g., Gershuny and Pahl 1980; Handy 1984). Handy, for instance, makes use of a colour-coded model to identify three 'shades' of economic activity in addition to the formal, or white, economy. There is thus the grey economy (based upon domestic and voluntary work); the mauve economy (deriving from marginal and part-time micro-businesses on the fringes of the formal economy); and the black economy (based upon illicit or undeclared activities of individuals and small businesses). In each of these economies, it can be argued, forms of small business either operate or have the potential to develop.

In the grey economy of domestic work, labour is unpaid and uncounted in financial terms but, according to Rose (1983), upwards of 50 per cent of the population's labour-hours can be spent in such activities. Although businesses in the normal sense will not operate from within this sphere, it is an area where potential business ideas and practices can be developed and 'tested' before moving into those economies where these goods or services will be bought for money. The ability of individuals to turn unpaid domestic work into the basis of a business activity has been claimed to be linked both to changes in the formal economy which have increased the leisure time and spending power of most groups, and to developments in domestic technology which have allowed people to acquire tools, and often skills, that were, in previous years, the preserve of 'professionals'. The pages of *Employment Gazette* and the small business columns of newspapers are not short of accounts of individuals who have turned hobbies or domestic chores into successful businesses, examples

92

being home cleaning and valet services, domestic appliance main-tenance, and interior design and decoration. Thus, skills learned and practised in the grey economy can, in theory, be transferred, as a form of small business, into the money-based worlds of either the formal, mauve or black economies. Such transference, how-ever, is not as straightforward as has often been assumed. In the first place the ability of individuals to develop potential businesses within the domestic economy will be conditioned by their access to resources such as money, knowledge and time. Such resources are unequally distributed and it would be surprising if those with greater access to them did not find the process of business formation and transference easier than those without. Second, there is the problem of marketing a business based upon work that would normally be done in the grey economy. For such activity to be a commercial success it is necessary for there to be customers who are able and willing to pay for something which, if pressed, they could in all probability provide for themselves. In this respect such businesses may be highly vulnerable to cyclical fluctuations in the formal economy, such that when disposable income shrinks potential customers may prefer to service themselves rather than pay someone else.

The mauve economy is one possible avenue for the development of a business conceived in the grey economy (as well as for non-domestic businesses). This is the home of what are best termed 'micro-businesses' – very small, generally run by a single person from home, and frequently part-time:

> These businesses are usually too small to need to be registered for VAT. They are the 'miscellaneous services' of the govern-ment statistics – if they ever get into the statistics . . . . They are not necessarily breaking any law or regulation [c.f. the black economy described later] because tax on the self-employed is collected in arrears, after the first year of trading, but such businesses do not keep PAYE accounts . . . . They are therefore hard to spot and count. They are betwixt and between the formal and informal economies, a respectable fringe.
> (Handy 1984:46)

Thus apart from being very small, a feature of businesses in the mauve economy is that their proprietors are unlikely to be dependent on them for their entire subsistence. On the one hand, micro-businesses may be run on a part-time basis either to supplement earnings from other work in the formal economy (either as an employee or self-employed), or to supplement the earnings of a spouse or partner within a domestic group. The latter is an option that would seem to appeal to some women as a means of contributing to the 'family wage' without disrupting perceived family commitments to the extent demanded when working for an employer (according to the GHS data [Curran and Burrows 1988:67; Chapter two of this book] over half the female self-employed work for less than twenty hours per week at their businesses). On the other hand, the government's Enterprise Allowance Scheme, which gives formerly unemployed individuals £40 a week for one year to subsidize business start-up (see Chapter seven), has undoubtedly facilitated the initial operation of many small businesses that would, without such assistance, have been unviable as full-time ventures. It seems, therefore, that businesses operating in the mauve economy may provide an effective means of supplementing income but offer only limited prospects as a source of subsistence in their own right. Here again, the ability to capitalize on the opportunities available in the mauve economy is likely to be more easily available to those already in possession of resources than to those without them (Pahl 1984). Indeed, where mauve economy businesses are run in a subsidized fashion (either by another wage or government payments) this may pose a threat to other small businesses in the formal economy, as wage costs in the former can be reduced to a level that would not be viable in the latter where business income is the sole source of livelihood. Once more there is the prospect that the better resourced will undermine the efforts of those who try to run marginal businesses without such a resource 'cushion' (Gill 1989).

The black economy provides one alternative to the mauve and formal economies. Here, entrepreneurial activity is of an illegal nature, either because it subverts social security or taxation law (by not declaring earnings from entrepreneurship) or because the nature of the business activity itself is illegal (e.g., dealing in drugs, or prostitution). The former activities, which may be termed 'evasive' entrepreneurship, have been seen by some writers to be related to levels of state welfare provision:

> differences in the role of the state in various European countries help to account for variations in the significance of the ... 'black' ... economies. In Britain, Italy and France, for example, governments have failed – by comparison to those in Scandinavia – to establish effective employment and industrial legislation, and to provide adequate state-funded health and welfare services. Further, they have failed to prevent rapid increases in unemployment over the past decade. As a result, those who are unemployed or on low incomes are often forced to 'get by' and

'to make ends meet' by trading in the black economy .... As such the black economy in these countries constitutes a seed-bed for business start-up. Similar opportunities are relatively restricted in those countries where the state regulates economic activity in a more rigorous fashion.
(Scase and Goffee 1987:7)

Even in the state-dominated societies of pre-*perestroika* Eastern Europe, however, black economy entrepreneurship is able to succeed. Grossman, for instance, describes the 'underground entrepreneurs' of the USSR who not only organize and promote production on a substantial scale (usually producing consumer goods), but also employ labour, obtain materials and distribute their produce widely. Such businesses 'are capitalized by the entrepreneurs and bought and sold privately at capitalized values that presumably reflect their expected profitability discounted for risk' (Grossman 1985:258).

In the UK, however, 'evasive' (as opposed to criminal) entrepreneurial operations in the black economy are likely to be of a more irregular or temporary nature. They may take the form of 'cash-in-hand' jobs undertaken as and when the opportunity arises, or the means of supplementing income derived from state benefits or low-paid employment where to declare black economy earnings would be to risk losing benefit or tax concessions – the so-called 'poverty trap'. For many in this position, however, black economy entrepreneurship is probably a temporary expedient to be abandoned once employment or better paid work is secured, rather than a potential business development. This is especially likely to be the case with those trying to avoid the poverty trap, as their business activity will invariably be hampered by under-capitalization and covert operation, hence, low profitability and little long-term viability.

In addition to evasive entrepreneurship, however, the black economy is also home to various forms of criminal business activity which may have a much more organized and enduring existence (it should be noted that evasive and criminal entrepreneurship are not mutually exclusive – individuals may practise both simul-taneously or move between the two as and when the opportunity arises [Hobbs 1988:140ff] – but neither is there any necessary reason for participation in one area to lead to participation in the other). One of the most recent studies of this kind of entrepreneurial activity is Hobbs's ethnography of working-class men in East London (Hobbs 1988), in which he produces a seven-fold entrepreneurial typology ranging from 'clients' (the entrepreneurially unsuccessful and marginal) to 'the Holding Elite' (those who have been entrepreneurially successful and established for themselves a secure, lucrative and [mainly] legal position in the labour market). For present purposes, however, it is Hobbs's 'in between' entrepreneurial types that are of most interest. These include the following: the Grafter; the Jump-Up Merchant; and the 'I'm a Business Man' (Hobbs 1988:141).

Grafters are 'unskilled and semi-skilled individuals who, despite their lowly position in the labour market, are able . . . to carve out an autonomous space based on entrepreneurial ability; a space that cushions and insulates the "grafter" from some of the more insidious effects of low-status employment' (Hobbs 1988:147). This entreprenerial ability is usually turned towards the task of 'fiddling' the employer via more or less elaborate forms of thieving (e.g., misrepresenting goods in stock records, deliberately damaging goods and selling them on at more than scrap value, etc.) which, none the less, involve not inconsiderable feats of 'business' planning both at the operational level (i.e., actually carrying out the fiddle) and in terms of finding customers for the 'acquired' goods, negotiating prices, and establishing the 'good-will' and credibility necessary for long-term 'trading' (Hobbs 1988:151).

Unlike the Grafter, whose entrepreneurial abilities are exercised from within the framework of conventional employment, the Jump-Up Merchant 'negotiates a living by partaking in any activity that proffers pecuniary reward without engaging him in the normative contractual arrangement suggested by employer–employee relationships' (Hobbs 1988:155). The range of criminally entrepreneurial activities available to the Jump-Up Man (a name which apparently derives from the practice of robbing delivery trucks left momentarily unattended during a delivery) is clearly broader than that of the Grafter; in fact, the whole pattern of his 'business life' is more 'fluid', moving between legal and illegal opportunities without distinction. As an example, Hobbs cites some of the activities of his respondent, Jack:

> Flexibility and optimism are key characteristics of any successful entrepreneur and Jack is no exception. One night he attempted to rob business premises but was thwarted by security arrangements, and the one accessible article of worth was an ancient wooden ladder. The following day he became a window cleaner, the next day he decided he was scared of heights, and by the end of the week had sold the ladder.
> (Hobbs 1988:155)

In practice, it seems, the limitations of the Jump-Up Man's marginal position in the formal economy mean that the bulk of his livelihood will be derived from activities of a more or less criminal kind. He is, in Hobbs's words,' a kind of buccaneer, roaming the streets day or night free to plunder and prosper' (Hobbs 1988:155).

The 'I'm a Business Man' type represents a bridge between the primarily deviant and/or criminal entrepreneurship of the previous types and 'those for whom entrepreneurial activity can be linked to legitimate, that is non-criminal, activity' (Hobbs 1988:163). This type of entrepreneurial action is based upon facilitation, the broking of goods and services (of virtually any kind) for those who have something to offer and those who want to buy. Acting in the capacity of an agent, no distinction is made by the Business Man between legal and illegal business:

> [He] is able to apply his skills to a range of situations, the scope of which encompasses those illegal activities that require presentational skills and verbal dexterity as opposed to physical commitment of a thief or robber. The 'I'm a business man' applies his occupationally accrued skills to confidence tricks, selling cut-price jacuzzis, and most spectacularly to the 'corner game' in equal measure.
> (Hobbs 1988:165)

What is clear from Hobbs's account of working-class culture in East London is the variety of ways in which entrepreneurial action can be operationalized, even within the black economy. Whilst he makes no claims of generality, and indeed develops his types specifically within the framework of a singular cultural context, there is no reason to suppose that versions of these entrepreneurial types could not be applied (albeit in less vivid terms) in localities other than East London. Small business, it seems, is not only to be found in the formal economy: a consideration of different levels and shades of economic action considerably broadens this category of activity. These 'business' ventures may be marginal in economic terms (although the black economy has been characterized by many as representing a substantial loss to the Exchequer) and their existence may be unstable and short-lived, but, as Hobbs's account so vividly reveals, their sociological significance is substantial, in that they can serve as an important means of livelihood and identity for the individuals and communities involved.

Alternative forms of small business activity, however, do not only take place outside the formal economy. Usually it is assumed that businesses operating in this latter arena will exhibit 'conventional' forms of ownership and organization, that is, as independent enterprises based on principles of sole ownership or the limited liability company. There are, however, other organizational and legal forms of business that are becoming more prominent amongst small firms. The two principal forms are producer co-operatives and the franchised business.

Despite a long history going back to the eighteenth and nineteenth centuries, producer co-operatives have grown in number particularly rapidly throughout the late 1970s and 1980s. In the UK in 1975 there were only some thirty co-operatives but by 1986 this number had expanded to well over 1,000, the majority being small enterprises (Cornforth 1988:10). In addition to co-operatives themselves, the 1980s have also seen the formation of some eighty funded co-operative support/development organizations (CDOs) charged with promoting and assisting the development of worker co-operatives. Even with this assistance, however, the rate of formation of co-operatives relative to other forms of small business remains very low at between 200 and 300 formations per year. The majority of these small businesses, not surprisingly, have fewer than ten members and, according to Cornforth (1988) operate in the margins of the economy, typically in the service sector (retailing, catering and distribution) or in craft-related industries and light manufacturing.

Before examining those factors which contribute to the formation rates and performance of co-operatives it is necessary to realize that this form of small business may take a number of different forms, depending upon the objectives of, and opportunities available to, those involved. In an attempt to clarify these differences Cornforth (1986) has produced a five-fold typology of worker co-operatives which can be summarized as follows.

1 *Endowed co-operatives* These are firms that have been 'given' by their original owners to their employees, shares usually being held in trust for the workforce. Such organizations are likely to be relatively secure in an operational sense, having arisen from established and already successful businesses. The usual motivations behind the formation of such co-operatives may range from moral idealism to a concern to safeguard the existence of the business in the absence of a 'family heir'.

2 *Worker buy-out co-operatives* This form of co-operative would come into being as the result of a workforce buying out the original owners of a business whilst that business was still successful. Given the not insubstantial resources necessary for such a transition to be accomplished, and the high level of prior commitment required amongst co-operators (without the goading influence

of immanent job-loss), this type of business seems unlikely ever to account for more than a tiny proportion of co-operatives formed.

3 *Defensive co-operatives* These are formed by employees of a business which has closed, in an attempt to preserve jobs. This type of co-operative is often a last resort after other forms of action have failed, a situation which may be reflected in subsequent difficulties associated with attempts to revitalize a business invariably in deep financial trouble.

4 *Alternative co-operatives* These represent a conscious and explicit response on the part of participants to construct an alternative form of working to that of conventional capitalism. Such co-operatives have a strong sense of moral purpose and emphasize democratic ideals and production for social need rather than profit alone. According to Cornforth (1986) this is the most numerous form of worker co-operative in the UK today, with examples found particularly in wholefood retailing, book selling, printing and some 'professional' areas.

5 *Job creation co-operatives* These are generally a response to high levels of unemployment and have been encouraged by governments and the co-operative development agencies as one means of getting unemployed people into jobs. The assumption behind such encouragement is usually either the belief that co-operation is ideologically more attractive to those disenchanted with conventional forms of business activity as a result of unemployment, or the view that the participatory nature of co-operation gives support to those who, alone, would not have the confidence to start a business. With the alternative co-operatives, job creation co-operatives account for the bulk of business growth in this area over recent years. These two forms will, therefore, be examined in more detail.

The recent growth in alternative co-operatives would seem to owe a great deal to the emergence of Green politics in the post-1960s decades (see Chapter one). According to one exponent of 'alternative enterprise' (McRobbie 1982:84ff) these co-operatives have been started mainly by young people concerned with changing lifestyles, and giving practical expression to the principles of smallness, simplicity, capital-saving and non-violence.

Not entirely unconnectedly, some feminists have also utilized this mode of business operation:

[They regard] their business ventures as part of a broader collective struggle to overcome, and eventually alter ... [male-defined] rules. Consequently their businesses are not geared primarily to profit-making and any surplus which is generated is regarded as a resource which can be used to further the interests of women. The intention is to create a social and economic environment within which an alternative life-style can be pursued, while at the same time, providing services needed by other women.

(Goffee and Scase 1985:99)

Such ideas have gained increasing momentum in most Western societies, resulting in the strengthening of existing co-operative support networks and increasing their amenability to alternative co-operative principles. Thus, alternative co-operatives have received assistance not only through the CDOs but also bodies such as the Industrial Common Ownership Movement (ICOM), the Workers' Education Association, the Open University, Workaid, and Commonwork (McRobbie 1982), not to mention the (then) Manpower Services Commission's Co-operative Enterprise Programme (Watkins and Chaplin 1986). Nevertheless, despite the growth in popularity and support, this type of small business faces a number of problems more or less closely associated with its organizational objectives.

These can include the tendency for alternative co-operatives to be located in markets where profits are generally low (e.g., wholefoods or bookshops), an absence of (or even ideological aversion to) formal training in technical and business skills, a preference for labour-intensive technologies, an emphasis on social rather than technical superiority as an organizing principle, and, frequently, a deliberate decision not to maximize profits at the expense of social objectives. (As will be seen later, not all these problems are restricted to alternative co-operatives). In summary, then, it seems that alternative co-operatives are largely a practical response to ideological discontent, manifested on a number of human/ecological fronts, with the nature of work and organization in advanced industrial societies. Whilst this impetus is unlikely to decrease in future years, it remains an open question as to how long such businesses can flourish, as they ultimately must, within an economy whose logic co-operators regard as socially unsound, before the tensions between market pragmatism and moral idealism become intolerable.

Job creation co-operatives, on the other hand, more closely resemble conventional small businesses in terms of their organizational objectives, and their emergence has been viewed by some commentators as a rational response by groups of individuals to the experience of unemployment. In this respect the idea of encouraging job creation co-operatives has found favour with a broader constituency than those sympathetic to the Labour and Green movements. Indeed, for supporters of the Enterprise Culture this form of co-operative, purged of any quasi-socialist ideals, fits well with the doctrine of 'popular capitalism'. Rainnie (1985:164), for instance, quotes George Jones, Chief Executive of the National Co-operative Development Agency, as claiming a coincidence between the co-operative way of running a business and the philosophy of the Thatcher government, on the grounds that co-operatives extend the Tory ideal of a job-owning democracy, and make people more realistic and responsive to market forces, prepared to take wage cuts when necessary and not go on strike. Thus, as a potential source of job-creation such enterprises have remained on the public agenda. Nevertheless, even for co-operatives driven more by economic pragmatism than moral idealism, serious difficulties remain. Co-operatives, even if not guided by socialist principles, require some system of democratic control and it may be that those who seek this route as a 'last chance' alternative to unemployment will have little experience or knowledge of forms of co-operative democracy (unlike the founders of alternative co-operatives, for whom such matters are a conscious and prior focus). Watkins and Chaplin, for example, report their experiences of running a co-operative enterprise programme:

> A considerable surprise was the frustration and confusion created by the even-handed approach to alternative constitutions. Many had started believing there was only one type of co-operative. They may have had difficulty grasping the conceptual and practical differences between each ... many participants had not before seriously questioned their own motives for starting a co-operative, nor thought through the administrative and policy implications.
> (Watkins and Chaplin 1986:218)

Another potential problem is the likelihood of a shortage of managerial and other technical skills, particularly as this type of co-operative formation may be a last resort for those whose lack of marketable 'employment skills' has ruled out other alternative avenues (Aldrich and Stern 1983). Finally, and as a result of the previous points, there is all too often reduced efficiency and unrealistic expectations. The danger is that in the enthusiasm to encourage any potential avenue of job creation, some may be seduced to begin ventures which have little hope of success and, as a result, exacerbate their original difficulties by adding business failure to other disadvantages.

Clearly, small co-operatives of whatever sort, will face many of the same problems as other small businesses. As Rainnie has put it: 'In the final analysis they have to compete to survive. And they have to survive in a world that is not of their own making' (Rainnie 1985:163). In facing these problems, however, the options available to small co-operatives are frequently more constrained than those of conventional businesses.

Cornforth (1988) suggests that there are three important barriers to co-operative development in the UK. The first of these is the predominance of materialistic and individualistic values which limit the appeal of co-operation to potential entrepreneurs, since such a form of organization is not in their material interests. This view receives some support from Watkins and Chaplin (1986:220ff), who, on the basis of their experience running small business training courses, use a model of entrepreneurial development (Timmons *et al.* 1977) to compare the entrepreneurial tendencies of co-operative members with those of other types of small business founder. Their tentative conclusion is that co-operative members are likely to exhibit a lesser degree of 'fit' with the characteristics of a 'successful entrepreneur' than are other types of conventional small business founder.

Second, Cornforth suggests that co-operatives are economically disadvantaged, in that there are often limits upon growth and expansion. These may result from fear of losing the 'sense of community' associated with a small-scale operation, but also from the practical difficulties involved in, say, taking over a non-co-operative business and assimilating it to co-operative ideals. Cornforth's third barrier is, of course, the legal restriction which prevents co-operatives from issuing external shares.

Finally, co-operatives face barriers to growth imposed by their overall inability to compete effectively with larger capitalistically organized businesses. Bennet (quoted in Cornforth 1988:12) makes this plain in an account of co-operatives in the shoe manufacturing industry where, it is suggested, they have failed not because of their inefficiency but rather because they have been squeezed out of the market as their potential outlets have been acquired by competitors. Co-ops have been unable to grow to a sufficient size (being unable to acquire other firms) either to set up their own outlets and have the strength to obtain a decent bargain with monopolistic buyers or to provide the range and flexibility of production available from large competitors.

On the basis of an analysis of the successful Mondragon group of co-operatives in Southern Spain, Cornforth (1988) provides a number of suggestions aimed at helping small co-operatives in the

UK. These suggestions run counter to the accepted UK wisdom regarding small business start-up (namely, that entrepreneurship is an inherently individual attribute, that assistance should be given to small firms generally, and that start-ups in any economic sector should be encouraged) and focus instead upon the prospects for the 'institutionalization' of entrepreneurship.

> Perhaps the most important point to emerge from Mondragon is that the entrepreneurial process is often too complex and important to be left entirely to the individual or small group of entrepreneurs. A great deal of expertise is concentrated in [the co-operatives' bank, the CLP] . . . and other support institutions . . . which any group wanting to found a co-operative can draw upon . . . . The bank is not in business to maximise profits, its goals centre on the economic and social development of the Basque region . . . . Clearly businesses in which it invests have to be viable but can be selected for their potential to create jobs more than purely for profitability . . . . Finally, Mondragon's strategy is not to support isolated, individual businesses, but to establish integrated systems of businesses. In this way the co-operatives can achieve economies of scale through having central services and joint ventures. This puts them in a better position to compete with larger businesses.
> (Cornforth 1988:17)

The extent to which the lessons of Mondragon can be transferred directly into a UK context is open to question, but there can be little doubt that this approach points towards a mode of small business start-up that is at least worthy of serious consideration. It certainly offers an alternative to the more individualistic approaches to co-operative development which concentrate either upon changing participants' attitudes towards the co-operative ideal (Woolham 1988:33ff), or upon programmes of formal education in business skills, both of which appear highly unpredictable in terms of successful outcomes. Similarly, it goes a stage beyond the informal, and often very tenuous, support networks offered by conventional CDOs.

Regardless of their type, therefore, it seems that the path to small business success through co-operation is not an easy one. Not only are there problems of finding capital to start an 'unconventional' form of business (frequently resulting in undercapitalization) and lack of business and/or technical skills on the part of participants, but also the day-to-day difficulties of contending with a pattern of authority and control which is likely to be unfamiliar and potentially stressful to many members. Indeed, this latter point reflects an established criticism of co-operatives formulated by the Webbs in the early years of this century to the effect that democratic patterns of ownership and control were ill-adapted to coping with the demands of the market, resulting either in increasing inefficiency and self-exploitation amongst co-operators, or the degeneration of co-operatives into conventionally managed business as the principals consolidate their power and ambitions. Whilst there remains a good deal of doubt as to whether such a fate is inevitable (Woolham 1988), the literature on small co-operatives does provide instances where precisely such processes do occur (e.g., Watkins and Chaplin 1986).

In many respects, franchising appears to offer a form of small business organization that avoids the sorts of economic problems exhibited so extremely by small co-operatives. At first sight franchising seems a simple enough idea. It has certainly been promoted as a way of owning and running a small firm without the risks usually attendant upon the independent trader, as the provider of the franchise offers not only a tried and tested business idea but also a comprehensive back-up and support service.

In fact, however, franchising is less clear than it first appears and there remains considerable debate as to whether or not franchised outlets are genuinely independent small businesses or whether they are, in practice, no more than branch outlets for a large company. To assess this debate it is necessary to understand something of the background to franchising, its development in the 1980s, and the implications of this for those who run franchised businesses. According to Stanworth and Curran, a franchise is defined as comprising a 'contractual relationship between a franchisee (usually taking the form of a small business) and a franchisor (usually a larger business), in which the former agrees to produce or market a product or service in accordance with an overall "blueprint" devised by the franchisor' (Stanworth and Curran 1986:157). This relationship is a continuing one, in which the franchisor provides general advice and support in the form of research, development, marketing and advertising services, in return for which the franchisee pays a royalty based on the level of turnover and/or a mark-up on supplies purchased from the franchisor. Finally, the franchisee provides the initial capital for the outlet and is legally independent of the franchisor.

There is, of course, nothing new about franchising: it has been used for many years by petrol companies and brewers as a distribution mechanism for their product. By the 1980s, however, the franchising business in Britain had become one of the most buoyant small business sectors in the economy, with annual sales through franchised outlets totalling around £3.8 billion in 1988, an increase of 23 per cent on the previous year (Churchill 1988:viii). There are, apparently, around 244 franchise systems operating in the UK, composed of around 16,000 units. The expansion of franchising is clearly the product of complex forces, but there can be little doubt that part of its success is attributable to the raised profile of small business generally and the attractiveness to those instilled with the desire to 'be their own boss' of a 'ready-made' small business opportunity. According to Churchill the severe recession of the 1980s also played a part by creating a pool of would-be entrepreneurs 'who had tasted the bitterness of failure with a large organisation but who, more importantly, had significant redundancy payments available to finance a franchise operation' (Churchill 1988).

The attractions of franchising, of course, do not appeal to the franchisee alone. For the franchisor this system is not merely the selling of a good business idea; it is also a strategy of business expansion which can be highly effective at the same time as minimizing capital and management costs. This appears to have proved particularly popular as a means of economic expansion for tertiary service operations characterized by labour-intensiveness and geographical dispersion, since operational control and the responsibility for the employment and control of staff can be decentralized. However, in addition to the direct interests of the franchisor in stimulating this form of business activity, there has also been a growing involvement of the clearing banks and government agencies in financing franchising. Most banks now provide a 'franchisee financing service' which not only lends start-up capital but will also assess the status of the franchisor. Similarly, those contemplating buying a franchised business can receive support from the Enterprise Allowance Scheme, the Loan Guarantee Scheme, and the Business Expansion Scheme. In financial terms it would seem that these bodies regard franchising as a relatively 'safe' target for business lending, at least when compared to other forms of small business venture.

If the boom in franchising can be attributed to the coincidence of strategic growth potential in tertiary industries, entrepreneurial zeal stimulated by high unemployment, and the willingness of financial lenders to encourage this form of business activity, this still leaves unresolved the question of whether or not the franchisee is a genuinely independent small business.

This question has been addressed by Stanworth and Curran (1986), who distinguish between two dimensions of franchisee independence: formal and operational. Formal independence refers to the nature of the contractual relationship between franchisee and franchisor. Their study of four franchise systems revealed that although the formal contract between the parties tended to be closely prescribed in favour of the franchisor and was frequently offered on a 'take it or leave it' basis, this was not always perceived as being strictly enforced.

> For instance, findings from both franchisors and franchisees suggest that the contract, although central in a formal sense to their relations, is not permitted a similarly explicit position in their day-to-day relations. For example, franchisors not infrequently have to pursue franchisees for their monthly statements or royalty payments. But this rarely involves an explicit reference to the franchisee's contractual obligations. Instead the appeal is usually framed in terms of the need for administrative efficiency and coached in the form of informal, personal pleas for co-operation from the franchisee.
> (Stanworth and Curran 1986:166)

Operational independence, on the other hand, refers to the everyday practice of the business operation, in recognition that no contract, however detailed, can dictate all aspects of practical business conduct. Franchisors, for instance, felt that they had less control over franchisees than would have been the case with a conventionally managed outlet. They had, they felt, to adopt a more persuasive style of management and to exercise direct or close control only in cases of extreme difficulty. Reservations were not held only by the franchisors, however. Those of the franchisees were reflected in the membership and formation of franchisee associations, either established by the franchisor to act as a forum for the exchange of views between the two parties, or an independent body established wholly by the franchisees with the intention of increasing their bargaining power with the franchisor. Overall, Stanworth and Curran conclude that franchisee independence at the operational level is clearly manifest in several significant areas of decision-making. Whilst both franchisors and franchisees accepted that the latter had overall responsibility in practice, franchisees were the only ones who could effectively make many of the everyday decisions. Indeed, they suggest, it is doubtful whether franchisors would ever want to make some of these decisions even if they claimed the ultimate right to do so (Stanworth and Curran 1986:172).

Nevertheless, the conclusion of these writers is that when compared to the conventionally independent small business, the franchised concern is less independent at both the formal and operational levels. They do qualify this assertion, however, by pointing out that such differences in independence are relative rather than absolute, to the extent that a good many formally independent small businesses may have as little, or even less, freedom from larger customers than has the franchisee from the franchisor. Thus they suggest that to dichotomize the distinction between franchised and conventional small businesses is misleading: for any small firm, independence is not an 'all or nothing' quality but is highly variable depending on the nature of the markets served and the type of business. As such, it seems that franchisee operations are, at least so far as Stanworth and Curran are concerned, entitled to admission to the wider small business fold.

From a point of view which emphasizes employment relations in franchised establishments this would seem to be an acceptable characterization. Workers in franchised outlets are employed by the franchisee, not the franchisor, and the former generally has complete control over the setting of wages and conditions of employment. In this respect it is to be expected that such terms and conditions will reflect those current in other small (independent) businesses operating under similar conditions. Trade unions, however, have expressed concern that the conversion of formerly centralized businesses into franchised operations can result in workers being disadvantaged as a result of the change of employer. In the case of Don Miller's Hot Bread Shops, for example, where there were recognition agreements with the bakers' union, BFAWU, in company-run outlets, the adoption of franchising resulted in 'check-off' arrangements (for payment of union subscriptions directly from wages) being terminated by the new proprietor (usually the previous manager), with the result that the union found it increasingly difficult to retain these small, isolated groups of members (*Labour Research* August 1986:19). Similarly, it has been claimed that franchising represents a means by which the management of a business can abdicate its responsibilities for employee welfare, exposing workers to a higher risk of exploitation in small firms, which are difficult for unions to organize and regulate. The shop workers' union, USDAW, for instance, has been alarmed by the Dairy Trades Federation's moves to use franchising as a last-ditch attempt to halt the decline in bottled milk sales by offering employees the option to take redundancy and then use their redundancy money to buy back their round and operate it on a self-employed basis. This, they claim, is 'simply getting individuals to take the risk on behalf of the dairies, and maybe pay the price for the lack of long-term strategy for the industry' (*Labour Research* August 1986:19).

Both co-operative and franchised small businesses represent non-conventional forms of business activity that have grown in importance throughout the 1980s. In many ways, however, these two types could not be more different: whereas franchised organizations are closely tied to a larger company which can provide support in times of crisis, co-operatives are all too often isolated, both from other co-operatives (at least in terms of more than moral support) and from conventional sources of finance and expertise. Perhaps not a little ironically, though, it may only be through the establishment of effective support networks of the sort available to franchisees that co-operatives will be able to flourish. Franchising may, in fact, have some lessons to teach those who argue for the institutionalization of entrepreneurship along Mondragon lines.

Clearly, there is significant variation in the levels of economic activity engaged in by small businesses and in their organizational forms. The notion of different 'economies' is a useful device for understanding such differences provided it is remembered that the boundaries are by no means clear-cut or easily identifiable in practice, that businesses may frequently move between them (not necessarily in an evolutionary manner), and that individuals or businesses may operate simultaneously in different economies.

But it is not only in the level and nature of their economic activity that small businesses differ. Another significant axis of variation centres upon the technological sophistication of this activity. In particular, a growing amount of attention is being attracted by the apparent distinctiveness of small businesses operating in the fields of new and high technology, and to the role which these play in advanced industrial societies. Indeed, the claims made for this type of small enterprise are such as to merit further consideration in the following chapter.

Chapter six

Small business, new technology and innovation

The notion that small firms are a significant force for technological change and innovation has become something of an accepted truth for many politicians and small business proponents. A popular image of the high-tech small enterprise, run by a scientist-turned-entrepreneur, has captured the imagination of many and has been bolstered by the cases of the 'Cambridge Phenomenon' and Silicon Glen in the UK, and Silicon Valley and Route 128 in the USA. The image has developed to embrace workers in these small firms as white-coated 'boffins' engaged in original creative activity in clean and pleasant laboratory surroundings. As so often in the world of small business, however, the image has assumed a clarity out of all proportion to the reality it claims to reflect. As will be seen in this chapter, the claim that high-technology small businesses are in some sense the vanguard of a revolutionary revitalization of the economy is one that must be treated with a good deal of caution.

As the debate about small businesses and technological change has developed a number of distinct theoretical 'foci' have emerged, each of which places a different emphasis upon the processes involved. To date, the earliest and most influential has been the 'industry life-cycle' approach, which has given rise to some of the more optimistic claims for the role of small business in the process of technological innovation. A second orientation has focused upon the role of regional and locational dynamics in stimulating the founding and success of new technology-based small businesses. And, third, the most recent contribution to this debate has been provided by the so-called 'community dynamics' model. These approaches share a common feature in that their primary focus is upon those processes which contribute to business/industry formation and growth rather than the internal dynamics of small, new technology-based firms. The latter, however, has been addressed, by what may loosely be termed 'labour process'

Figure 5.1. Advantages and disadvantages of small and large firms in innovation

	Small firms	Large firms
Marketing	Ability to react quickly to keep abreast of fast-changing market requirements.	Comprehensive distribution and servicing facilities. High degree of market power with existing products.
Management	Lack of bureaucracy. Dynamic, entrepreneurial managers react quickly to take advantage of new opportunities and are willing to accept risk.	Professional managers are able to control complex organizations and establish corporate strategies. (Can suffer an excess of bureaucracy. Often controlled by accountants who can be risk-adverse. Managers can become mere administrators who lack dynamism with respect to new long-term opportunities.)
Internal communication	Efficient and informal internal communication networks. Affords a fast response to internal problem-solving; provides ability to reorganize rapidly to adapt to change in the external environment.	Internal communications often cumbersome; this can lead to slow reaction to external threats and opportunities.
Qualified technical manpower	(Often lack suitably qualified technical specialists. Often unable to support a formal R&D effort on an appropriate scale.)	Ability to attract highly skilled technical specialists. Can support the establishment of a large R&D laboratory.
Finance	(Can experience great difficulty in attracting capital, especially risk capital. Innovation can represent a disproportionately large financial risk. Inability to spread risk over a portfolio of projects.)	Ability to borrow on capital market. Ability to spread risk over a portfolio of projects. Better able to fund diversification into new technologies and new markets.
Patents	(Can experience problems in coping with patent system. Cannot afford time or costs involved in patent litigation.)	Ability to employ patent specialists. Can afford to litigate to defend patents against infringement.

Source: Adapted from Rothwell 1986:117
Note: ( ): potential disadvantages.

theories which have adopted a broader and more critical understanding of the effects of new technologies. Each of these
approaches will be examined in turn below.

The industrial life-cycle thesis finds its earliest origins in
the work of Kondratiev (1935) and Schumpeter (1939) (more
recently expounded by Freeman [1983; 1984]), which argues that
capitalist development is punctuated by 'long waves' of boom
and slump. A crucial feature of such explanations is the impact
of bursts of radical technological innovation. In this context
some writers have argued that the 1970s and 1980s have witnessed
a new and continuing 'technological revolution' based on
innovations in micro-electronics and information technology
which is generating a 'creative gale of destruction' along
Schumpeterian lines (Keeble and Kelly 1986:76). Put crudely,
Schumpeter suggested that entrepreneurs and small businesses
play a significant role only as economies or industries develop,
during which period they fulfil an innovative function. Later,
however, they become marginalized as the consolidation of
innovation becomes dependent on the huge economic resources
possessed only by large organizations. In a revision of this
idea Rothwell (1986) emphasizes a link between large and small
organizations in the process of innovation which he terms
'dynamic complementarity'. As the name implies, dynamic
complementarity suggests that large and small firms possess
distinct characteristics that, together, are capable of producing
synergistically innovatory results. Rothwell's summary of these
differences is shown in Figure 5.1. The key point derived by
Rothwell is that in terms of innovation the advantages of large
firms are associated with the relatively greater 'material' (i.e.,
financial and technical) resources available to them, while those
of small firms are 'behavioural', namely their capacity for
flexibility and adaptability (Rothwell 1986:118). Using data from
the Science Policy Research Unit, Rothwell concludes that
although the bulk of British industrial innovations have been
produced by large organizations, 'the most promising feature
is the increasing innovative efficiency of SMEs [small and
medium-sized enterprises, defined as those with fewer than 500
employees]; given their relative lack of research and development
resources, they have performed remarkably well' (Rothwell
1986:125).

On the basis of case studies of the semiconductor and CAD
(computer-aided design) industries in the USA and Europe,
Rothwell outlines the 'Schumpeterian evolution' of these industries
in terms of dynamic complementarities thus:

Existing large firms provided much of the basic, state of the art technology, venture capital and technically skilled personnel which were essential to new technology-based firm start-up; the new technology-based firms provided the risk-taking entre-preneurial drive and rapid market exploitation.
(Rothwell 1986:131)

The choice of these industries is, of course, significant, since micro-electronics and computerization have been widely held to be the epitome of new technology. There are, indeed, two key inferences commonly associated with the 'industry life-cycle' thesis which are derived from these industries (both points, however, have been prone to exaggeration, frequently by those unacquainted with the complex and detailed empirical work conducted in this area): first, that micro-electronics and computerization represent a 'new wave' of technological evolution set to revitalize and regenerate the flagging fortunes of industrial capitalism, and, second, that in the early stages of this developing cycle – that is, the immediate future – small firms are destined to play a key innovatory role.

Out of this concern the 'regional dimension' arises as a 'natural' corollary, given the observable tendency towards agglomeration characteristic of the micro-electronics industry in both the USA and UK, where industrial centres have developed in clearly defined spatial clusters (Oakey 1984:42ff). The two factors held to be of crucial importance in explaining the localized 'clusters' of small high-tech firms are, first, the proximity of major scientific research institutions such as universities or government establish-ments and, second, a high-quality local residential environment capable of attracting and retaining the highly mobile research scientists and entrepreneurs. Both factors, according to Keeble and Kelly (1986) are illustrated by the principal UK 'high-technology complexes': Cambridge, the M4 Corridor in Berkshire, and 'Silicon Glen' in central Scotland. Such clustering not only has implications for regional employment and economic buoyancy but also for the formation of new small firms. Thus,

The crucial role of highly qualified research engineers and scientists in these technological changes, coupled with often relatively limited financial barriers to entry, permits the break-ing away of such individuals to establish their own independent firms to exploit commercially valuable product and process innovations.
(Keeble and Kelly 1986:77)

This, as much as anything, is held to explain the pattern of geographical concentration so characteristic of new high-tech small firms. The Cambridge case has been most thoroughly researched and is frequently cited as a glowing example of the future potential of high-technology small business. For these reasons it is worthy of closer scrutiny.

The concentration of small high-tech businesses in the Cambridge area has certainly been dramatic, from 100 in 1974 to 322 in 1984, three-quarters of the latter figure being indigenous independent enterprises. In 1984 these firms employed 13,700 people and had a turnover of £890 million, all the more striking given that 70 per cent employed fewer than thirty people. In addition, each company had, on average, eight graduates, the latter constituting one third of all employees (Segal Quince 1985; Rainnie 1989:145f). Indeed, the so called 'university effect' was equally marked among new business founders. According to Keeble and Kelly's study, 30 per cent of founders had come directly from academic research, 50 per cent had PhDs, and over 80 per cent had some form of higher education (Keeble and Kelly 1986:96ff). The same study also revealed a low average age amongst founders: 77 per cent were under 35 and 16 per cent under 25. The majority of these entrepreneurs had 'spun off' from small and medium-sized, rather than large, firms in the Cambridge locality (and, of course, from the University research departments).

Impressive though the case of Cambridge is, the evidence to suggest that the performance of small high-tech businesses is the vanguard of a general process of economic revitalisation is less hopeful. On the one hand, the apparently startling performance of small high-technology firms needs to be put in a wider context. In terms of employment generation, for example, Storey (1985:224) has pointed out that in the decade up to 1981 in Cambridgeshire, the supposed centre of high-tech activity, only five jobs in every 100 were created by new firms of any description, the numbers being even lower elsewhere. Also the 'regional effect' seems to be largely self-reinforcing, tending to benefit already prosperous regions rather than those in decline, to the extent that the latter not only possess less than their proportionate share of high-technology sectors but the companies based there tend to be less innovative than their counterparts in south-east England (Shearman and Burrell 1988:89). In short, new high technology-based small firms, whilst performing well in the short term, cannot be claimed either to have drastically contributed to economic regeneration on a widespread scale or to be the guarantors of long-term stability and growth. Unfortunately this rather 'weak' conclusion has tended to be underplayed. As Wildsmith (1984:21) has commented of those who advocate extensive support for small firms as industrial innovators, their enthusiasm is often the result of a predeliction for the small business solution rather than a consideration of the balance of the evidence. This criticism is echoed by Shearman and Burrell (1988), who provide a critique of the position adopted by, in particular, Rothwell (Rothwell and Zegveld 1982) and Oakey (1984), focusing upon their supposed conceptual confusion, definitional laxity and consequent tendency to overstate both quantitatively and qualitatively the positive effects of small business activity.[1] In essence they suggest that writers such as Rothwell *et al.*, in their enthusiasm to establish a positive role for SMEs in industrial rejuvenation, have oversimplified both the concept of industrial rejuvenation itself and the associated distinction between new technology-based firms (NTBFs) and high-technology SMEs. With regard to the former, they claim, it is necessary to distinguish between 'industrial regeneration' (which involves 'managed' innovation in already established industries intended to develop new products based on relatively new technologies for established markets) and 'reindustrialization' (which refers to the emergence of wholly new industries 'characterized by technologies, products and markets so novel as to be still in the process of definition' (Shearman and Burrell 1988:90)). It is conditions of industrial regeneration that will favour Rothwell's notion of dynamic complementarity but it is not NTBFs that are involved in this relationship but rather high-technology SMEs.[2] And the difference between high-technology SMEs and NTBFs remains, according to Shearman and Burrell, profound:

> high technology SMEs possess comparatively sophisticated organisational structures and manufacturing processes. Market-oriented rather than technology led, they have clearly targeted applications and customers for their products and operate on the basis of price considerations and commercial realism. In our view, NTBFs, by contrast, are relatively rare. They have small simple organisational structures and clear, strong, active university links. Technology led rather than market oriented, NTBFs operate on the basis of ad hoc problem solving with one, or at most two, products at the prototype stage, their applications and markets as yet uncertain and ill-defined.
> (Shearman and Burrell 1988:90)

It is thus in the context of reindustrialization that small firms can play an important role, but not in an unconditional manner.

In terms of their prospects for employment generation NTBFs do not themselves appear to offer much promise. First, their very scarcity limits the contribution they can make. But second, and more interestingly, Shearman and Burrell claim to have identified a distinct business motive among proprietors of NTBFs (some caution is necessary here as this conclusion is derived from a very small sample in a specialized industrial sector – medical lasers). They suggest that many entrepreneurs see their objectives in terms of being bought out by larger organizations seeking product diversification. Hence they plan neither for growth in employment terms nor even on investment returns but rather in terms of enhancing their appeal to larger acquisitive organizations. If this is so, then it calls into question the effectiveness of proposals such as Oakey's which recommend that government-linked equity should be used as a mechanism for stimulating small new-technology firms in developing areas on the grounds that this would 'protect' such firms from the 'asset-stripping acquisition behaviour of larger firms' (Oakey 1984:158f). For Oakey it is taken for granted that such take-overs are hostile and resisted by the small business but, following the logic of the former argument, to prevent such acquisitive behaviour might be to remove the original motives for business start-up.

Such matters, it seems, cannot be entirely explained either by a perspective which concentrates upon the assumptions of growth through competition (as implied in the notion of dynamic complementarity), nor by a strictly regional analysis, but must also be comprehended within a 'social' model of industrial development. The notion of 'community dynamics' is intended to provide such a model (Shearman and Burrell 1987). Four stages in the process of industrial evolution are thus recognizable: the community; the informal network; the formal network; and the club. These stage-posts arise from the development of the social relationships which form within a particular industry, relationships which develop both between organizations and between individuals, the actions of whom may constitute a major dynamic force for development. The significance of this approach for the study of small business is that it focuses upon relationships within specific industrial contexts and avoids the use of arbitrary statistical definitions (of the SME sort) and their associated tendency to conflate important organizational differences within a single apparently homogeneous category. For community dynamics the emphasis is upon issues of style, strategy and structure rather than size per se:

analysis at the 'industry' level allows [NTBFs] to be conceived more broadly in terms of a cohering network of social relationships stretching beyond the confines of the actual company boundaries. Our image of an emerging industry, therefore, is one based on the notion of a 'community' ... this model suggests both a geographical dimension including physical proximity and a normative dimension involving some shared social values and ideologies expressed through the medium of social and organisational interaction within the 'community'. (Shearman and Burrell 1988:94)

Such an approach has the added merit of allowing researchers to investigate the qualitative dimension of employment in NTBFs as well as quantitative growth/demographic issues and, in this respect, the findings of Shearman and Burrell reintroduce themes discussed in Chapter four. It will be recalled that there attention was drawn to the employment practices of small new/high technology firms in relation to their reliance upon highly qualified skilled labour.

The community dynamics research reveals that NTBFs tend to operate with dual labour markets characterized by a core of professional staff (engineers, doctoral students, academics, etc.), apparently enjoying other sources of income, non-routine jobs and relatively non-hierarchical working environments, and a 'peripheral' labour force recruited for production work, typically enjoying little security of employment (frequently being made redundant in the event of the hoped-for take-over). The conclusion is that 'NTBFs role in job generation has little to commend it either in terms of quantity or quality' (Shearman and Burrell 1988:97). They are, it seems, unlikely to offer high-quality employment to any but a handful of exceptionally qualified individuals; for most terms and conditions will not be markedly different from other small businesses operating in more established industries. Indeed, the pattern of industrial relations described here would seem to fit quite adequately into the category of benevolent autocracy discussed in Chapter four.

In other respects though, NTBFs operating within the context of product innovation, developing and bringing to the market wholly novel products and technologies, are not typical of most SMEs (high-technology or otherwise). For most other small businesses the effects of new technology are more likely to be felt through more or less radical 'process innovations' – that is, with the application of new technology components to existing production processes or the introduction of completely new technological processes to produce the same or similar products more efficiently. The concern with process innovation, of course, goes beyond the realm of the so-called sunrise industries and into fields affected by micro-processor-based technological change via application rather than development.[3]

Process innovation within small businesses, however, has attracted relatively little research attention. In part this is explained by the belief among some researchers that 'the impact of process innovation on small firm *growth*, and certainly on *employment*, can be termed marginal' (Oakey 1984:14 emphasis added). Such beliefs, however, are founded upon the assumption that the relevance of small business is to be assessed primarily in quantitative terms, i.e., how much employment it will generate, or revenue it will produce. It pays less attention to the qualitative dimension of small business activity, particularly as this affects employment relations. There is now evidence to suggest that small firms in both services (Treadgold 1988) and manufacturing (Poutsma and Zwaard 1988; Griffith and Dorsman 1986; Campbell and Warner 1987; Edwards 1989) are not unaffected by process innovations. A study of 331 SMEs in services and manufacturing by Griffith and Dorsman for example, found that 82 per cent had introduced some form of new technology into their organizations, ranging from computerization of payrolls and accounts to CAD and CAM (computer-aided manufacture) systems (Griffith and Dorsman 1986).

It is within the context of process innovations that labour process theories become relevant. Indeed, they have given rise to one of the most persistent debates to have developed within industrial sociology over the past two decades. This debate, which emerged with the publication of Braverman's *Labour and Monopoly Capital* in 1974, originally began as an investigation of managerial strategies in relation to the deskilling of labour via the organization and control of work. The role of new technology in the deskilling process quickly emerged as a key issue and has been a much-debated source of contention, with opinion divided between two broad camps.[4] On the one hand are those who claim the centrality of a tendency towards the enskilling of labour: new technology creates a fundamental and rationally enlightened transformation in the nature of work and employment, and an expansion of skills based upon computer-literacy and science, reflecting the contraction in traditional manual occupations and the growth in 'mental work'. Directly opposed to such theories of enskilling are those claiming that the principal thrust of new technology is to deskill and degrade labour, with a concomitant emphasis upon dehumanization, work intensification, stress and hazard caused by new technology.

With both opposing theories there is a common weakness which derives from their high level of generality and the associated need to extrapolate unilinear tendencies from heterogeneous and selective comparative data. The result is all too often a form of technological determinism which posits that a simple change in technology will necessitate a corresponding change in both production and social relations. Indeed, the tendency to present novel features of social change as evidence of a widespread 'trend' encourages a neglect both of detail and those factors that indicate continuity with existing forms of organization. For these reasons such 'general' theories of technological change have come under attack from those who favour more empirical and open-ended approaches. It is notable that when the issues raised by new technology are looked at in detail much of the supposed novelty tends to disappear. What emerges is a picture of technological change which is characterized both by diversity and complexity (Goss 1988) such that outcomes are contingent upon a range of factors pertaining to the circumstances faced by specific work locations (Edwards 1989). Such an approach is particularly suited to the study of technological change within small firms as it does not minimize the heterogeneity which is so characteristic of small business, a heterogeneity which macro-level 'trend theories' necessarily diminish, thereby marginalizing the role and nature of change within such organizations.

An investigation by this author into the effects of technological change on small firms in the general printing industry revealed the presence of both deskilling and enskilling effects, these being linked to a complex of inter-related factors, as will be shown later (Goss 1988). This analysis, like that of Shearman and Burrell (1988) starts at the level of the industry rather than with the notion of firm size per se. This is important, because although technological change in print has taken the form of a general shift from letterpress to offset lithography, the precise impact of this change has been far from uniform, reflecting the very different technical requirements of different industry 'segments'. In practice, the general printing industry is not homogeneous but is composed of a number of broad market areas distinguished in terms of product ranges, output volume, production technology and labour requirements, two such areas being 'quality colour (sheet-fed) printing' and 'high-volume (web-fed) printing'.

The dominant technology employed in high-quality colour printing was, even into the 1970s, a combination of letterpress and photo-mechanical methods. By the 1980s, however, this had almost totally been replaced by offset lithography, computer-composition and computer-aided colour-scanning and plate-making. In the seven firms investigated (employing between four and thirty-two employees), though, the new technology in both press and composing rooms remained complex and dependent upon a range of delicate manual adjustments to control crucial aspects of reprographic quality. Not only did operators need to be fully conversant with the technology itself, they had also to know exactly what to look for in the finished product so as to be able to make running adjustments and ensure consistent results. Thus, although the new technology differed radically from its predecessor, the knowledge and control of the operator remained crucial factors, a fact confirmed by all the employers in this field. Similarly, skilled workers who had made the transition from old to new technologies expressed the view that although different, the level of skill required by both was roughly comparable. In high-quality colour printing, then, there existed a situation in which employers were dependent on the genuine skills of their employees. But, in addition, many of the employers interviewed held views which, at least in relation to craft skills, were broadly sympathetic to the concerns of craft workers (if not always to their union), a sympathy grounded in many of their own experiences of 'working at the trade' before starting in business. Typically this led to a proprietorial craft ideology which recognized the need to retain and develop employee skills in order to safeguard standards of quality which isolated businesses in this sector from the ruthless price competition characteristic of low quality, semi-skilled instant print. Certainly, in the cases studied, new technology had not been directly responsible for job losses through redundancy, and existing letterpress craft employees had been retrained to operate the new technology. Thus, in this context, it seems more appropriate to speak of 'reskilling' rather than deskilling or enskilling.

Turning to high-volume web printing (i.e., from a continuous web or reel of paper), five firms were studied, ranging in size from 60 to 220 workers, all of which were involved exclusively with the production of periodicals and magazines and which used techniques similar to those for newspaper production. Prior to the introduction of offset lithography, metal type had been set using Linotype machines and printed on large, labour-intensive rotary presses. The adoption of new technology introduced considerable changes in all fields of production. In the composing departments the old metal type had been replaced by sophisticated computer terminals with full-page make-up facilities. In the press room the new machines, apart from being considerably faster, were amenable to sophisticated systems of computer control and monitoring, facilitated by the long production runs and standard-ized nature of the product, which simplified or eliminated many of the previously time-consuming manual adjustments. The large presses used in this type of production are composed of a number of interconnected 'units' through which the continuous web of paper passes. With computer control the adjustments for every unit can be made from a centralized workstation, whereas previously at least one skilled machine minder, with assistants, would have been responsible for making adjustments to each individual unit. In spite of these significant changes the immediate effect on the organization of the labour process appeared to be limited. In none of the firms had new technology resulted in redundancies (although numbers of skilled workers had declined through 'natural wastage'). Neither had it led to a loss of skilled status for craft workers. In part this could be accounted for by the strong paternalistic ethos which characterized proprietorial ideology in these 'family firms' but, ultimately, the preservation of skilled manual status seemed to owe more to the effectiveness of union pressure than to the employer's genuine dependence upon a large skilled labour force or paternalistic benevolence. Certainly the new technology had the potential both to deskill and destroy significant numbers of craft jobs and, objectively, many of the traditional printing skills had vanished. As one employer, half-jokingly, commented; 'A monkey could run that machine!'. Indeed, interviews with craft workers revealed a widespread feeling of sadness that their long training in the 'mysteries' of the printer's craft was now of little practical use. They recognized that their jobs were cleaner and lighter than previously but, as one pointed out, 'Its not really a compensation for the loss of your skill and the satisfaction of knowing that you were in control of a whole job.' Paradoxically, however, management appeared reluctant to drive home the deskilling potential of new technology. Contributing to this reluctance was the relatively strong position of the craft union. These firms were large enough to support cohesive union chapels, closely linked to the union at regional level (a consequence of their relative importance in an industry composed mainly of very small firms), and prepared to challenge any attempt by management to undermine the position and status of skilled workers. Throughout the industry's history, skilled workers have organized to exercise exclusive control over their craft (Musson 1954; Child 1967). Such exclusive strategies (usually in the form of apprenticeship regulation, craft demarcations and the pre-entry closed shop) have been aimed against employers and unskilled workers alike, with the intention of retaining control of the labour process in the hands of craft union members (Zeitlin 1979). The craft union's success in this respect has been largely dependent upon its ability to enforce sanctions against recalcitrant employers, either by a withdrawal of labour or the practice of 'blacking' an offender's suppliers and customers. In the case of web printing the power of the craft union was enhanced by the nature of the product and its market. The 'perishable' nature of magazines and the stiff competition between titles, meant that employers were unwilling to initiate action which might jeopardize production and, hence, lose large contracts. Indeed, for management the dominant strategic concern seemed to be the preservation and safeguarding of stable market position, incorporating a belief that union demands should, if at all possible, be accommodated rather than challenged directly. Under such conditions the craft union was in a relatively strong position to protect the skilled status of its members in the face of an objectively deskilled technology. Here again is an instance where little support is lent either to the deskilling or enskilling thesis. What does emerge, however, is some support for the conception of skill as a 'social construction', built upon the material basis of union power in the workplace and labour market. In this respect, the social organization of new technology appears better understood as the outcome of the relative balance of power between, and strategic concerns of, capital and labour within this particular industrial sector.

Similar findings emerge from a study of the effects of CNC (computer-numerical-control) automation within small engineering firms in the Netherlands (Poutsma and Zwaard 1988), which emphasizes the dual possibilities of such technologies either to deskill or enskill, depending upon the situation faced by particular businesses. Poutsma and Zwaard identify a number of factors which influenced the ways in which CNC introduction affected operators, ranging from a desire by management not to jeopardize the loyalty of operatives by turning them into 'button-pushers' (resulting in an effective enskilling by involving operatives in programming the machines), to cases where the tasks of operating and programming were separated and the formal training of operatives in programming resisted on the grounds that this might enhance their position in the labour market thereby increasing the company's vulnerability to labour turnover. Even in those cases where the result of CNC application was the enskilling of operatives, however, Poutsma and Zwaard point to some undesirable effects:

> The change-over from machine operator to working at computer controlled machines is experienced as considerable; especially when control and programming tasks are a substantial part of the new job content. In those cases a shift from manual to mental work occurs, which can be accompanied by mental stress. A stress situation may occur during the initial period when the equipment is being introduced. This involves feelings of greater risk and responsibility. Although the switchover is often viewed as a promotion, this is seldom reflected in employment conditions.
> (Poutsma and Zwaard 1988:42)

Interestingly, in those cases where operatives were involved in the programming of the new machines these writers point to a pervasive tendency for recruitment to be 'internal' – i.e., from amongst the operatives themselves – and for a disinclination to employ 'ready-trained' operators from the external labour market or to recruit those with 'higher' level qualifications. This not only bears upon the findings discussed here, but also those of Griffith and Dorsman in the UK, discussed earlier, which revealed that 94 per cent of SMEs using information technology and 93 per cent of those using manufacturing technologies had trained their existing employees in its use (Griffith and Dorsman 1986:32ff).

In some areas of manufacturing, however, the speed and increase in product complexity brought about by technological change have necessitated the 'bringing in' of specialist new technology workers, a necessity that can create problems for small businesses. In a study of twenty-six manufacturing sites (65 per cent being SMEs) where micro-electronics had been incorporated into products, Campbell and Warner point to a general shift in the importance of electronics design and development specialists and describe the effect upon one of the smaller mechanically based companies that had moved further and further into electronics:

> The company saw something of a 'cultural rift' between laboratory-based graduates and the rest of the company . . . . At the outset, over 90% of the workforce had been blue-collar. Over the last few years this had decreased to 60%. With micro-electronics applications increasing since 1980, the electronics department had begun to marginalise mechanical engineering. The number of graduates in the former discipline had increased

from 3 to 35 in 5 years, with no corresponding growth in the other.
(Campbell and Warner 1987:93)

Ironically, the creation of such a 'cultural rift' would seem to be a precondition of business success for enterprises in this area of production, not only because of product-development requirements but also as a means of attracting increasingly scarce well-qualified specialists, i.e., by offering non-routinized development work without the 'technical ceiling' associated with standardized production and perceived by such specialists as limiting career opportunities. And in this respect smaller firms appear to be at a distinct disadvantage compared to their larger counterparts, as a growing shortage of graduate engineers and scientists restrict the recruitment possibilities of all but the largest and most prestigious engineering companies. This, in turn, perpetuates the dominance of larger firms in electronics, since few small firms can provide both interesting work and an adequate career structure for ambitious recruits (Campbell and Warner 1987:95).

Interestingly, one solution to this immanent skill shortage identified by Campbell and Warner as appropriate to small firms re-emphasizes the possibilities of retraining existing staff. They suggest that it should be possible for small firms to train technicians and craft labour (or those educated to HNC level) for jobs that would be the preserve of graduates in larger companies. Indeed, they argue that such retraining has an additional advantage in that technicians tend to have a broader base of experience and be more flexible than graduates.

Such findings do little to confirm the existence of any inherent link between small business and technological innovation. On the contrary, the study of small firms and new technology testifies more to the complex and multi-dimensional nature of this relationship. Storey's point is well made when he remarks on the fact that

For every Racal, Sinclair, etc. there are probably several thousand small firms who have no wish to innovate, and a good deal more who are incapable of so doing. In this, as in many other respects, the small firm in the electronics or instrumentation industry bears no resemblance to a firm of similar size in the furniture, printing, food-processing or dressmaking industry. The grouping of firms on the basis of size, is probably less meaningful in terms of innovation than any other aspect of the debate over the merits of small and large firms.
(Storey 1982:35)

A more adequate alternative to the 'size-oriented' approach has been shown to be one which concentrates upon social relationships at the organizational and industrial levels. Within such a perspective it is neither size nor new technology alone that are the decisive variables but, rather, the relationship between these and other intervening factors. In other words, the new technology–small business relationship is viewed as the outcome of a process of 'negotiation' (in the interactionist sense) through which organizational actors, as individuals and in various types of coalition, interact to influence particular organizational outcomes within the constraints and opportunities presented by structural factors (Clark 1988:10). On the basis of the research discussed in this chapter the following factors (not listed in order of priority) merit consideration in attempts to explain the impact of new technology:

1 *Managerial ideologies and strategies* In small businesses the outlook and actions of the proprietor (or his or her agents) will be of particular importance in defining the role and possibilities of new technology. Examples of these discussed in this chapter include the maintenance of craft standards in colour printing and the conscious courting of the acquisitive attentions of larger organizations found by Shearman and Burrell amongst the proprietors of NTBFs.

2 *The nature of the work skills involved* To understand fully the impact of new technologies upon the skills of those who work with them, or are recruited to do so, it is necessary to appreciate that skilled status incorporates a 'social' dimension capable of being constructed or destructed independently of the objective 'technical' content of a particular job. In web printing, for example, the ability of craft workers to defend their skilled status in the face of a deskilled technology had allowed them not only to safeguard their relatively privileged position but also to benefit from technological change by claiming enhanced terms and conditions for having to master new skills (even though in practice their jobs were less demanding than before). In contrast, however, Poutsma and Zwaard described the operation of CNC machines as a process over which operators had relatively little control, management being able to define the status of the new process unilaterally by a process of trial and error. Thus

the management has, simultaneously with the introduction of the first CNC machine, given higher wages to the operator involved, because the CNC work was thought to be more

difficult. With subsequent operators this procedure was dropped, because the operation of the machine turned out to be less difficult than was initially supposed.
(Poutsma and Zwaard 1988:42)

It is to be expected that situations of the latter kind will be common in most small firms, where union organization of the kind present in the printing trade is markedly absent.

3 *Labour market conditions* These are likely to have significant effects upon all aspects of new technology and technological change. Thus, in the case of NTBFs and reindustrialization, highly specialized labour markets for scientific and technical personnel of the sort found only in the proximity of key university and research establishments appear to be a precondition for growth, and a partial explanation of the agglomeration feature of such activity. For high-technology SMEs, on the other hand, labour market requirements are less geographically limited but still dependent upon the availability of highly qualified personnel, for whom they have to compete, often on unfavourable terms, with large enterprises. In some cases this may result in the limitation of diversification and expansion for small firms and the necessity to 'upgrade' less well-qualified employees. Indeed, there appears to be a general tendency in the labour market behaviour of smaller businesses, certainly in the area of new technology applications, to retrain existing employees to operate new technology rather than to seek already trained or new workers in the external labour market.

4 *Product demand factors* Here consideration needs to be given to stability and volume of demand and independence from customers and/or suppliers. Where small high-technology firms are heavily dependent upon a few large customers, for instance, the latter may be able to demand levels of flexibility, performance and price which severely limit the competitive position of the smaller business:

In the information-technology sector, increasing customer awareness, combined with a slow-down in demand growth, has led to firms having to provide a wider range of services to secure a contract. In one illustrative instance ... the small company in question had not only to customize software for its clients on an individual basis, but also had to install the equipment over a long period, and train customers' staff in its use .... In the event the company went bankrupt through cash-flow problems.
(Campbell and Warner 1987:89)

125

Alternatively, the stability of product demand (or lack of it) may be not only a key factor in deciding whether a business should adopt a new technology process, but also be a vital component in managerial justifications for changes in working practices among employees. Equally, as in web printing, the need for management not to jeopardize output in a competitive market may allow employees to retain, or even enhance, their control of new technology processes.

5 *Organizational structure*   It will be recalled that Shearman and Burrell referred to differences in organizational structure between NTBFs and high-technology SMEs in terms of 'simple' and 'sophisticated' structures respectively. This would seem to parallel research which indicates that innovation is achieved most efficiently in 'organic' as opposed to 'mechanistic' organizational designs (Burns and Stalker 1961; Blau *et al.* 1976) and that such organic designs should operate most effectively on a small scale (Hull 1988). Put crudely, 'mechanistic' organizational structures refer to the type of 'classic' bureaucracy modelled by Weber (1978). Here there is a strict hierarchy of authority with clearly defined channels of communication from 'top' to 'bottom' and strict definition of individual responsibilities and work roles. 'Organic' organizations, on the other hand, are characterized by 'flat' structures, in that there are relatively few levels of hierarchy, and communication between and within levels is open and unconstrained by formal regulations. Burns and Stalker, according to Hull, suggest that 'employees in organic designs can better direct their expertise toward innovation if mechanistic barriers are reduced so that communications can take place rapidly on a face-to-face basis regardless of hierarchical chain of command, specialization of functions, centralization of power, or bureaucratic rules' (Hull 1988:393). This, of course, does not mean that all small firms, even NTBFs, will adopt such organic structures. As previous chapters have shown, small businesses may exist in many structural forms and there is the additional possibility that the openness and non-hierarchical nature of the organic form may conflict with proprietorial ideologies, particularly where a 'power culture' (see Chapter Four) has been fostered.

Taken together, then, these factors whilst not assuming the status of predictive variables do give some indication of the diverse dimensions of the small firm-technology nexus and complexity of their interrelation. This however has not stopped the small firm–new technology conjunction being blithely hailed by governments and small business proponents as the potential salvation of industrial capitalism and as the breeding ground for a new generation of small businesses.

Indeed, guided by this assumption small business in general has been bathed in the healthy glow of technological innovation, supporting an ideological climate in which political and economic support have been forthcoming regardless, and frequently in ignorance, of the real contribution made by small firms to employment and growth. It is to an investigation of state policies towards small business, therefore, that the next chapter is devoted.

Chapter seven

Small business policy

The rise to power of a right-wing Conservative Party under the leadership of Margaret Thatcher has, as seen in Chapter One, placed small business near the centre of the political agenda. As the present chapter will show, this has been reflected in a whole series of policy measures designed to foster, directly and indirectly, the formation and growth of small business. The affinity between the political and ideological positions of free-market Conservatism and small business will not be reiterated here in detail, but will be commented on as it is reflected in specific pieces of policy.

Small business policy, of course, is not an invention of the Thatcher government. In the UK its origins can properly be traced to the Bolton Committee which, established by a Labour government in 1969, presented its Report to the Conservatives under Edward Heath in 1971. According to Beesley and Wilson (1981: 254) the interest generated by the Report, as a result of its examination of the disadvantages suffered by small firms and its recommendations for remedial action by government, marked the starting point of what has now been nearly two decades of steadily increasing small business policy activity.

Whilst the Bolton Report was extremely reticent in approving any major form of positive discrimination in favour of small firms, it did point to the existence of policies that, albeit unintentionally, had the effect of discriminating negatively against the small business. Such past discrimination should be removed, the Report counselled, and care taken not to reincorporate similar practices into future policies. Both Labour and Conservative governments in the early 1970s appear to have endorsed these conclusions and geared their policy considerations first to 'providing an environment in which small business could thrive, free from interference of any kind', and, second, 'removing the discriminatory impact of existing legislation' (Beesley and Wilson 1981:258).

By the mid-1970s, however, the policy of the Labour government had taken a more interventionist twist, albeit of a rather low-key nature. In 1977 it appointed the Wilson Committee to inquire into the role of the financial institutions and the provision of funds for industry, including a study of the financing of small firms, which was published in March 1979. This proposed the establishment of small firm investment companies and a publicly underwritten loan-guarantee scheme. By comparison with what was to come, however, these measures appear moderate in the extreme. With the election of the Thatcher administration the steady stream of measures to assist the small business sector turned into a torrent, to the extent that this government claimed to have introduced 108 such measures over the period from 1979 to 1983 (Mason and Harrison 1986:225). These fall into three broad categories: finance; legislation and administration; and information and advice. Each of these categories will be considered in turn.

Financial measures have been many and varied but the following can be considered of greatest importance:

1 *Small Business Loan Guarantee Scheme* This is intended to supplement bank lending by guaranteeing repayment of 80 per cent of the loan. The intention of the scheme, which was first introduced in 1981, is 'to help banks and other financial institutions to lend money to small businesses for promising projects which would otherwise present too great a risk under normal terms, say due to lack of security or track record' (*Employment Gazette* August 1989:415). The guarantees cover one or more loans up to a maximum of £100,000 and are available for terms of between two and seven years; a premium of 2.5 per cent a year on the amount guaranteed is payable by the borrower. Since 1981 the LGS has covered lending of over £700 million to more than 21,000 small firms.

2 *Enterprise Allowance Scheme* Those who have been un-employed and receiving unemployment benefit for eight weeks can claim £40 a week for a year to offset the loss of benefit when starting their own business. Participants must invest at least £1,000 of their own capital in the venture.

3 *Business Expansion Scheme* This is intended to serve incorporated but unquoted firms looking for equity investment of under £50,000. Investors can deduct up to £40,000 in any one year from an individual's tax liability.

4 Other measures include the *Support for Innovation Programme* (also available to large firms), *Regional Development Grants* and *Regional Selective Assistance* (Owualah 1988).

On the face of it, evaluations of these policies appear generally favourable. In April 1989, for instance, the Loan Guarantee Scheme was extended indefinitely and the maximum sum available for advance increased to £100,000. This scheme has recently been evaluated by National Economic Research Associates (NERA) with summary results published in *Employment Gazette* as follows:

* The LGS does generate additional economic activity by allowing commercial banks to provide small firms with finance which would not otherwise have been available. In a sample of 106 small firms using the LGS between August and October 1986, NERA found that a little under half of the £4.18 million LGS finance raised would not have been raised by the firms in the absence of the scheme ...
* The additional finance attributable to the existence of the LGS among the sample firms was responsible for saving 140 jobs which would otherwise have been lost and for creating 220 new jobs in growing and new firms.
* Taking account of displacement effects which are difficult to estimate, perhaps 70 per cent of the additional activity in sample firms represented additional small firm sector activity ....
(Ridyard *et al.* 1989:417)

These findings, however, require some comment. The key concern in assessing schemes such as LGS is in terms of 'additionality' (i.e., an event which would otherwise not have happened), but here the detailed account of the NERA results is slightly less reassuring than the summary suggests. First, there is the methodological difficulty that the figures for additional jobs created are derived not from objective measures but from the opinions of borrowers on the nature of the markets in which they operated – hardly likely to be a dispassionate assessment! Second, whilst it is claimed that 70 per cent of jobs attributable as additional to LGS were also additional to the small business sector, this does not take into account displacement at the expense of large UK firms. When this is considered, 'measurable' additionality at the level of the economy as a whole was much lower, about 10 per cent (Ridyard *et al.* 1989:420). Finally, it needs to be remembered that these findings were generated at a time of high economic activity and relatively low interest rates. There is now mounting evidence that the persistently high interest rates of 1989 are having a severe effect upon small businesses with high borrowings. It remains to be seen whether large loans to high-risk ventures prove as beneficial to business success under changed economic circumstances.

Turning to the Enterprise Allowance Scheme, according to the

Manpower Services Commission's evaluation (Allen 1987), 76 per cent of businesses that had completed twelve months on the scheme were still trading six months later (i.e., six months after Scheme payments had ceased). Whilst this would appear to be a reasonably acceptable level of success, it should be noted that the MSC's figures seem likely to understate the real failure rate. The figures are based on a questionnaire response rate of 60 per cent from a population of 1,300, but no data on the status of non-respondents are provided in the report. It seems fair to assume that a not insignificant proportion of non-respondents would be failed businesses. In other words, it is likely that the sample is biased towards successful businesses. If this assumption is correct, the success rate could drop (in the 'worst case') to 60 per cent.

Indeed, when broken down, the results of the EAS are less spectacular in terms of their success, particularly in terms of creating jobs other than for the participant. At the eighteen-month period most of the businesses created appear to be very small, only one-third being registered for VAT. In terms of job generation, for every 100 businesses set up, ninety-one new jobs were created. But of these only thirty-seven were full-time, the rest being part-time (i.e., less than one-third of a full-time job per business). In addition, however, there is the likelihood that the EAS may affect the employment potential of existing businesses (a point not considered in the MSC evaluation). As the London and South East Regional Planning Conference report:

> The success of an EAS venture may however mean job loss from existing firms ... more than a third of EAS survivors [in a SBRT survey] said their success involved price cutting below competitors, whilst three-fifths of survivors said they had tried to take customers away from their rivals, rather than create new markets.
> (RPC 1987:6)

Returning to the MSC data, it emerges that the manufacturing sector created 41 per cent of full-time jobs but represented only 17 per cent of EAS participants, the bulk of whom were in the service sector (over 60 per cent). Survival rates in manufacturing, however, were below those for the less job creative service businesses (72 as opposed to 77 per cent). Indeed, the precariousness of many of the business started under EAS is indicated by the fact that over half of the failures occurred within a month of the last payment of the allowance.

Finally, it is worthy of note that business success under EAS did seem to bear some relationship to the resource advantages of those involved. Thus, survivors were more likely to be married or living as married and to have a spouse in paid employment, more likely to be male, less likely to suffer from ill health, to have experienced shorter periods of unemployment before starting a business, and to be older than non-survivors. In addition, fewer survivors than non-survivors would not have set up their businesses without the aid of the EAS; survivors were also able to invest, on average, nearly twice as much as non-survivors in the business (Allen 1987:i). In short, this would seem to confirm the findings discussed in Chapter Three, that those who enter business from a relatively advantaged social position have greater likelihood of success. This in itself must call into question the presentation of small business as a universal panacea for the problem of unemployment, since it seems that those who are most likely to find themselves unemployed are precisely those who also have the least chance of starting a successful business.

Thus, despite a wealth of publicity and highly favourable comment from Government spokespersons, debate over the effectiveness of small business policy continues. Storey (1982), for example, provided an early and sustained critique of small business policy, in which he attacked conventional justifications and pointed not only to dubious success rates but also to the potentially divisive effects at regional level. It was, claimed Storey, by no means certain that subsidising the formation of new firms would, on balance, benefit the national interest, as opposed to those who gain directly from such subsidies (i.e., intending or actual small business owners):

> Clearly, subsidies by government to those wishing to establish their own firms will result in an increased number of new firms and lead to an increased employment in the small firm sector. But subsidies to one group have to be raised by increased taxes or reduced reliefs to other groups, and it has never been shown that the *net* effect of subsidising small firms is to create more wealth in the community.
> (Storey 1982:205)

Indeed, this point formed the basis for Storey's claim that such policies would be regionally divisive. Taking into account a number of factors claimed to affect entrepreneurship (size of incubator firm, occupational experience, education, access to capital, barriers to business entry, and markets), Storey proposed what he termed an 'index of regional entrepreneurship' (Storey 1982:185), reproduced in part in Table 7.1. In terms of their innate entrepreneurial potential, regions can be grouped into three broad

Table 7.1 Index of regional entrepreneurship

Region	% in small manufacturing plants	% in large manufacturing plants	% going to degree courses	% without qualifications	Savings	Barriers to entry	Average score*
Northern	2	1	2	7	8	1	3.45
Yorks & Humberside	7	8=	6	4	5	4	4.64
E. Midlands	6	10	3=	6	10	6	6.09
E. Anglia	8=	8=	1	8	4	11	6.91
South-East	11	7	8	10	7	10	9.18
South-West	10	6	5	9	9	8=	7.64
W. Midlands	3=	3	3=	3	6	9	5.27
North-West	5	4	7	5	11	7	6.64
Wales	3=	2	10	1	3	8=	3.70
Scotland	8=	5	9	n.a.	2	3	5.11
N. Ireland	1	11	n.a.	2	1	5	4.44

Source: Adapted from Storey (1982:196)
Note: *Present table does not include Storey's figures for Occupational Class, Owner Occupation, and Disposable Income.

categories: at the top of this 'league table' is the South-East, followed by the South-West; at the opposite extreme the bottom places are occupied by the northern region of England, and Wales; between these two poles are the remaining regions. Extrapolating from these results Storey drew the conclusion that policies offering incentives to small firms and to individuals to start their own businesses were likely to result in take-up rates varying significantly between regions because of differences in entre-preneurial potential. In particular, those areas suffering the highest rates of unemployment were also those with the lowest entrepreneurial potential. As such, policies assisting small firms rather than large would risk being regionally divisive, as the biggest take-up rates would be in areas which were already the most prosperous – that is, such policies would generally favour the South rather than the North of England (Storey 1982:195).

However, later research by Mason and Harrison (1986:224ff) into the regional effects of four 'key' small business policies (the LGS, the BES, the Small Engineering Firms Investment Scheme [SEFIS], and the EAS) fails to reflect the clear-cut south–north dichotomy suggested by Storey. Although they find that the South-East, East Anglia, and the South-West have more recipients and a greater share of funds than expected (i.e., on the basis of their proportion of eligible applicants for each scheme), and that three of the 'peripheral' regions (Wales, Yorkshire–Humberside, and

Scotland) have lower than expected take-up rates, they point to greater variability in the other regions. There are, for instance, peripheral regions where the take-up of one particular scheme may be greater than expected, but where take-up of other schemes is low. Thus, Northern Ireland has the largest relative share of SEFIS but the lowest relative share of LGS and BES; the North-West has the highest take-up rate under LGS and EAS but less than its fair share of SEFIS and BES; and the North has more than its fair share of LGS and SEFIS grants but fewer than expected EAS participants and BES investments (Mason and Harrison 1986:247).

Whilst accepting that differences in regional entrepreneurial potential coupled with regional environmental factors may explain the broad contrast between the South-East, South-West and East Anglia and the other regions of the UK, Mason and Harrison point out that other explanatory variables are necessary to account for the variations in take-up of particular schemes between regions. Thus they draw attention to regional variations in knowledge of available schemes amongst small business owners, particularly likely if specific schemes are vigorously promoted only in certain areas, either by government or interested private-sector organizations such as banks or, in the case of SEFIS, machine-tool suppliers. Similarly, they point to the fact that some schemes may, in some regions, be 'crowded out' by the activities of other organizations. Where, for example, banks are more active in lending to small businesses – as is the case in Scotland – this may lessen the number of applications under LGS.

Mason and Harrison conclude that the regional disparities in the effectiveness of small business policies reflect a general lack of co-ordination between those policies intended to promote national economic growth and those attempting to reduce regional differences. Their solution is a compromise involving the creation of nationally available industry-aid schemes, in which the level of assistance varies according to regional 'need' and which would be capable of restricting the availability of certain schemes only to depressed regions (Mason and Harrison 1986:250).

The notion of 'selective' small business assistance has also been raised by Storey in his later work (1985:219ff; 1988). Accepting the findings of Mason and associates (e.g., Mason and Lloyd 1985) that the nature of the differences between entrepreneurs in different regions are often of a subtle and quite marginal nature but that they impact across a broad range of businesses within particular regions, Storey identifies a choice of two possible policy directions. Either policy has to aim to make relatively small improvements in small business performance over both a large number and a broad range of companies, *or* it has to be highly selective (Storey 1985:224); that is to say, directed towards encouraging the handful of firms which have the potential to expand and thereby to create jobs locally and change local attitudes and aspirations.

The choice for Storey is clear. The first policy direction – i.e., helping a wide variety of small firms – is, he claims, 'doomed to failure', destined to founder in the face of the sheer diversity of small businesses and business needs encountered. The only workable alternative is to discriminate in favour of those firms whose performance, per pound of public assistance, will have the maximum benefit for the economy.

> Hence the objective of small business policy has to be to increase *net* employment locally; in short it requires a policy of avoiding the losers and picking the winners within an expanding economy. 'Winners' in these terms will represent only a very small proportion of small firms.
> (Storey 1985:225)

However, as Storey *et al* (1988) have conceded, this type of discriminatory analysis is both expensive and time-consuming; they also admit that it may be difficult without the aid of hindsight to distinguish fast-growth firms from others (see Chapter two of this book).

Whilst the notion of targeting is appealing at an intuitive level and has the appearance of good sense, it has been further challenged on the grounds of impracticality by Hakim (1989a) who (on the basis of the MAS Business Line data discussed here in Chapter two) claims that there is no apparent or easily identifiable difference between fast-growth firms and others which could serve as the basis for selective targeting of aid at an early stage. She accepts that the three most likely characteristics of size, legal status and home/premises base are consistently associated with fast-growth small firms but points out that these are only probable characteristics of fast-growth small firms and that their possession is not, of itself, a guarantee that a business will be a fast-grower. In other words, the characteristics of 'winners' are not strictly exclusive to fast-growth small firms but are, albeit less frequently, also shared by many slow- or no-growth enterprises. For Hakim, then, the process of 'spotting the winners' amongst small firms in a predictive sense is far from certain. On the one hand, whilst the typical characteristics of a fast-growth small firm may be known, these cannot be used with any degree of certainty to distinguish this type of firm from the mass of slow- and no-growth enterprises.[1]

Turning now to legislative changes aimed at small business, the principal measures were first spelt out in the White Paper *Lifting the Burdens* (1985). This reflected the Conservative government's assertion that business in general suffered from an excess of restrictive and bureaucratic regulation, and that effective performance could only be achieved by the removal or 'reform' of such regulatory control. Many of the proposed 'reforms' have applied to businesses of all sizes, but there are two areas (not including changes in financial/tax thresholds and reliefs) where small business has attracted special treatment. These are the areas of health and safety at work, and employment protection (in the latter case the changes pioneered in the small business sector were subsequently extended to cover all businesses). Both areas are important as they continue to raise the problem, identified above, of the apparent mismatch between the findings of social scientific research and the espoused intentions of policy initiatives.

The approach to health and safety in *Lifting the Burdens* is an interesting one. It begins with the declaration that the government 'has no intention of down-grading health and safety standards either generally or in relation to small firms', but,

> Nevertheless there are a number of areas in which action can be taken to assist employers without any reduction in standards. These include:
> – raising the threshold of the requirements on employers to prepare a written safety policy from 5 to 25 employees ...
> – giving specific training to inspectors to increase their awareness of smaller firms' interests.
> (*Lifting the Burdens* 1985:22–3)

However, despite the statement of intent to maintain safety standards in small firms, it is difficult to see how the proposed policy changes – i.e., removing very small firms still further from statutory requirements and encouraging the implicit assumption that inspectors should treat small firms more leniently (what else can 'increasing awareness of small firms' interests' mean?) – can in any way safeguard this objective. Indeed, it should be remembered that small firms are less likely to recognize a trade union and thus more likely to deny employees the access to either a health and safety representative or the information so provided.

The rationale for the limitation of health and safety coverage is called further into question when considered in the light of available evidence. On the one hand, a government-sponsored survey (cited in *Releasing Enterprise* [1988:372], the 'follow-up' to *Lifting the Burdens*) appeared to show that employer demand for change was muted, to say the least: 'only a very small minority' of respondents thought health and safety and employment protection requirements burdensome.[2] On the other hand, the record of small firms in relation to health and safety, particularly to serious accidents and fatalities, does little to inspire confidence.

Nichols (1986:302), for instance, has made a convincing case for small firms being more accident prone (in terms of serious injuries and fatalities) than larger organizations. Put simply, his hypothesis seems to be that levels of industrial injury will be related to the intensification of labour associated (albeit in a complex fashion) with the operation of the business cycle and that, in turn, those most vulnerable to such intensification will tend to work in labour-intensive rather than capital-intensive sectors and to lack the protection of trade unionism. Such features, he suggests, will be more in evidence in SIC (Standard Industrial Classification) orders, where employment is skewed towards small establishments, and less in evidence in orders where employment is concentrated in large organizations. This pattern does indeed seem to occur in the figures presented by Nichols, represented in Table 7.2. The arrangement of this table allows it to be read from top left to bottom right, the highest injury rates being in leather and timber (both characterized by small establishments, low wage rates and low levels of trade union organization) and the lowest in shipbuilding, vehicles, and coal and petroleum (all with relatively high levels of unionization and wage rates, and large establishments). One interesting exception alluded to by Nichols is that of paper, printing and publishing. Here the injury rate is low but the proportion of small establishments high. To account for this apparent anomaly Nichols points to the exceptionally high union density of this industry, particularly amongst small firms in printing, and the relatively strong position of the print unions.

These findings appear to be borne out by health and safety statistics for manufacturing industry, cited by Nichols (1986) in a later paper (Table 7.3). There are, of course, two caveats to be added to this analysis of industrial injuries. The first concerns the fact that the tables refer only to *establishments* and not to *enterprises*. It is possible, therefore, that there may be a difference between rates of injuries in small independent businesses (i.e., enterprises) and those in small establishments (which could be part of a larger organization). Such a difference, however, is not amenable to analysis with the present statistics, and the best that can be said is that, in general, those industries with a high

Table 7.2 Employment concentration and average rates of change in fatal and major injuries, 1981–4

		Concentration of employment			
		*Pronounced employment in small estabs**	*Higher employment in small estabs***	*Lower employment in small estabs†*	*Pronounced employment in large estabs††*
SIC order					
XIV	Leather, leather goods and fur	17.78			
XIX	Other manufacturing		16.73		
IX	Electrical engineering			13.75	
XVI	Bricks, pottery, glass, cement		13.73		
XVII	Timber, furniture	13.62			
XIII	Textiles		11.90		
XV	Clothing and footwear		11.53		
V	Chemicals and allied			9.13	
XII	Metal goods		9.06		
VII	Mechanical engineering		7.85		
VIII	Instrument engineering		7.75		
III	Food, drink and tobacco			6.87	
VI	Metal manufacture			5.51	
XVIII	Paper, print and publishing		3.54		
XI	Vehicles				3.30
IV	Coal and petroleum products			−9.93	
X	Shipbuilding and marine				−11.55
	Employment concentration averages	15.70	10.20	5.10	−4.10

Source: Nichols 1986:300–1
Notes: * Over 50 per cent of employees in units employing 99 or less (Leather 66 per cent; Timber 58 per cent).
      ** Between 40 and 25 per cent of employees in units employing 99 or less.
      † Less than 20 per cent of employees in units employing 99 or less.
      †† Over 60 per cent of employees in units of 1,000 or more.
      For all manufacturing industries 25 per cent of employees are employed in units of 99 or less. Apart from vehicles (71 per cent) and Shipbuilding (63 per cent) the range of all other SIC orders for percentages of employees in units of 1,000 or more is from nil (leather) to 47 per cent (metal manufacture).

Table 7.3 Injuries by size of establishment in British manufacturing

Employment group	*Size injury rate (per 100,000)*	
1–19	117	
20–49	125	119
50–99	115	
100–99	86	
200–499	84	79
500–999	73	
1000+	74	

Source: Nichols 1989:63

concentration of small establishments also tend to have high concentrations of small enterprises. The second caveat is that the present data take no account of differences in technology, processes or workforce composition as these may affect injury rates. There are no easy answers to this problem, although it might be suspected that taking account of such factors would have a greater effect on the magnitude of the trend rather than its direction.

This pattern is repeated when attention is shifted to employment protection issues. In this area the government's position has been unshakable: namely, that employment protection legislation (in particular, the 1974 Employment Protection Act [EPA] and its successors) prevents small firms from employing more people because employers fear being unable to dismiss 'unsatisfactory' employees. This, it is claimed, has adverse effects upon the level of employment generally. In response to this perceived problem the 1980 Employment Act removed the right to complain of unfair dismissal from new recruits to firms employing fewer than twenty workers, until they had worked continuously for that firm for two years. (Under the provisions of the EPA this period had been reduced to six months, but subsequently extended to one year by the newly elected Conservative government in 1979; in 1986 the two-year period imposed upon small firms was extended to cover businesses of any size.)

In making these changes there can be little doubt that the government was acting both in line with its own belief that the balance of power had shifted too far away from employers, and in response to pressure from organizations claiming to be representative of small business interests. This point has been well made by Westrip, who has produced an impressive critique of surveys conducted by the National Federation of Self Employed and the Engineering Employers Association which served as the basis for the parliamentary case for the changes in employment protection coverage. Westrip's findings reveal these surveys to be riddled with elementary methodological errors and implicit bias, reflected in suspect samples, loaded questions and instructions to respondents, unjustified inferences and generally inadequate analysis (Westrip 1982:44ff). In the light of these criticisms it is difficult to take seriously the claim that these surveys revealed over 70 per cent of small businesses to be adversely affected by employment protection legislation.

As a counter to this distortion, Westrip points to two rigorous surveys carried out in the late 1970s by the Policy Studies Institute (PSI) (1977) and the Opinion Research Centre (ORC) (1978), both of which cast considerable doubt upon the simplistic view taken by policy-makers. The PSI survey, for instance, found very little sign that employment protection legislation was inhibiting industrial recovery by discouraging employers from taking on new people. Although this survey included a relatively small sample of very small firms, the summary of results provided by Westrip is of interest:

> where this study isolates the effects of legislation on small firms, it suggests that generally they fared better than their larger counterparts. The researchers did, however, suggest that the legislation was more *unpopular* in small firms, whilst having had substantially more influence upon practices of larger firms. Indeed, the researchers, whilst being sympathetic generally to the types of problems that such legislation could create, 'unequivocally' rejected 'the crude form of criticism' levelled principally by employer interest groups.
> (Westrip 1982:39)

The ORC survey (commissioned by the Department of Employment), on the other hand, was designed to study the effects of legislation specifically upon small firms. Its results, too, were far from unequivocal: over half the sample (54 per cent) had no direct experience of any aspect of the legislation; only 12 per cent said they had experienced and found troublesome at least one item from a detailed list of provisions; some respondents felt that employment law created difficulties for firms wishing to reduce their labour force, but 63 per cent said it made no difference. The researchers concluded that these 'results counter the suggestion that the legislation had some massive and widespread effect on small firms' (Westrip 1982:42–3).

As with other areas of small business policy, therefore, changes in employment protection legislation appear to have been made more in response to political expediency and 'pressure group orthodoxy' than on a balanced assessment of available evidence. As Westrip remarked, 'Whilst present policy appears to have in large measure reflected an ideological demand, it is questionable whether this will have any significant impact on levels of employment in the individual firm or across the small firm sector as a whole' (Westrip 1982:61). Indeed, the best that can be said is that these policy changes make it easier for employers to dismiss workers. That small business should have been in the vanguard for the removal of such protection is somewhat disturbing given their relatively poor record in relation to the incidence of unfair dismissal claims. Data for 1985–6, for instance, confirm the picture which emerged in the 1970s that 'the typical unfair dismissal applicant [was] . . . a male manual worker, not in membership of a union, who had been dismissed after a relatively short service by a small employer in the private sector' (Stevens 1988:659). Indeed, the 1985–6 results show that, despite shifting the onus of proof in favour of the employer at an industrial tribunal (Employment Act 1980), unfair dismissal applicants working in establishments with under ten employees had an above-average success rate at tribunal hearings (Stevens 1988:652). The implication would seem to be that small employers are more prone to dismiss workers unfairly than large organizations, and it could reasonably be argued that workers in small firms deserve more rather than less protection, particularly since the evidence to support the notion that such protection prevents job creation is questionable in the extreme.

The final broad area of policy initiatives to be considered is concerned with advice and information for small business. The provision of advice, guidance, education and training for small firms has grown phenomenally throughout the 1980s. Originally small business advice was provided primarily by the Small Firms Service (SFS). This was established by government in 1973 in the wake of the Bolton Report. It now has some 350 small business counsellors and in 1987–8 dealt with 266,000 inquiries and provided 39,000 counselling sessions. The Small Firms Service aims to provide information and advice both to those contemplating starting a small business and to already established enterprises. The work of the SFS has now been supplemented by the Training and Enterprise Councils (TECs), which, funded by the Training Agency (formerly the Manpower Services Commission), are locally based, employer-led organizations charged with co-ordinating industrial training needs. According to the *Employment Gazette* (March 1989:112), the inclusion of 'enterprise' within the TEC's jurisdiction recognizes 'that the small firm sector has played a major part in the regeneration of the British economy'.

Provision has also been made for small business training through the government's 'Business, Training, Growth' initiative launched in March 1989. This has made available funds of £55 million to assist small businesses in particular to develop training strategies for their employees and organizations. For example, up to £15,000 is available to firms with fewer than 500 workers to fund half the cost of employing a training consultant.

In addition to these central provisions there also exist a multitude of training courses for small business which have mushroomed in colleges, polytechnics and universities over the last decade and are only indirectly related to centralized small business policy. In terms of delivery, most operate independently under the auspices of the institutions concerned, although many are funded, in full or in part, by local and central government via a variety of 'enterprise initiatives'. Similarly, there can be little doubt that the stimulus to the growth of such courses, and the market for them, is in no small part a function of the high profile that the Conservative government has given to small business as an alternative to conventional employment.

In a recent review of provision in this area, Curran and Stanworth point to the existence of four distinct types of small business education: entrepreneurial education; education for small business and self-employment; continuing small business education; and small business awareness education. These are represented in Figure 7.1. Referring to the first category, Curran and Stanworth suggest that entrepreneurship should be defined as 'the creation of a new economic entity centred on a novel product or service or, at the very least, one which differs significantly from products or services offered elsewhere in the market in terms

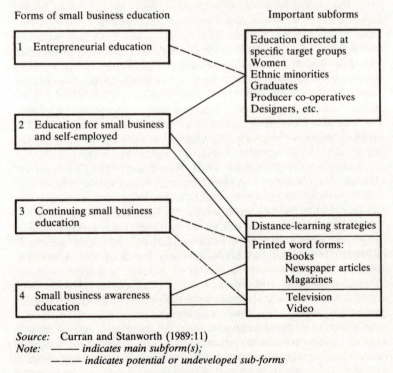

Forms of small business education   Important subforms

1   Entrepreneurial education

Education directed at specific target groups
Women
Ethnic minorities
Graduates
Producer co-operatives
Designers, etc.

2   Education for small business and self-employed

3   Continuing small business education

Distance-learning strategies

Printed word forms:
    Books
    Newspaper articles
    Magazines

4   Small business awareness education

Television
Video

Source: Curran and Stanworth (1989:11)
Note: ——— *indicates main subform(s);*
        – – – *indicates potential or undeveloped sub-forms*

Figure 7.1   Types of small business education

of content or the organisational configuration from which it emanates, or marketing' (Curran and Stanworth 1989:12). Not surprisingly, they find that education and training for this type of small business activity is virtually non-existent, perhaps even impossible, since there is no body of knowledge sufficiently well-developed to serve as the basis of a teaching programme. As entrepreneurship is a highly creative process it is even doubtful that conventional forms of small business education would be helpful, these being based on principles of order, rationality, predictability that are often far from the charismatic approach of genuine entrepreneurs. The second type of programme – education for small business ownership and self-employment – however, is a different matter. Here the intention is to prepare people for small business ownership. Such programmes are geared to providing help of a practical kind concerned primarily with the everyday skills and requirements associated with small business ownership, from preparing business plans and balance sheets to raising finance. These courses are by far the most common of those available, but despite their popularity there is little reliable research relating to their success rate in preparing individuals for small business careers. Indeed, Curran and Stanworth express some doubt about such courses on the basis that most tend to be short (increasingly a function of cautious funding decisions by one of the main financiers, the Training Agency) and over-general, ignoring important aspects of the experiential transition from conventional employment to proprietorship (Goss 1989). Such issues, according to Curran and Stanworth, would be most appropriately tackled through 'follow-up' courses of 'continuing small business education'.

Continuing education for small businesses represents the third type of programme and is acknowledged by Curran and Stanworth to be still in its infancy. Such programmes seem likely to be 'resource heavy', both in terms of time and the necessity closely to match course content to individual business needs (i.e., to escape from the over-generalized prescriptions of the previous type of programme). One possible solution is seen to be distance learning, but even here, experiments by the Open University have been less than encouraging (the Start Your Own Business course which aimed to attract 500 students per year attracted only 400 for the entire period 1985–7, with less than 5 per cent of those who started actually producing a business plan [Curran and Stanworth 1989:17]). Despite these difficulties, Curran and Stanworth remain convinced of the importance of this type of education. This is confirmed by results from two studies of small firms in engineering and related industries (Blackburn and Hankinson 1989) which showed small firms to be in urgent need of training if they are to make the most of available opportunities for growth and development. These writers, however, remain pessimistic about the prospects of rectifying this situation given a consistent attitude amongst the small business owners studied to regard training as an expense rather than an investment.

The final type of programme is small business awareness education. This is aimed at increasing the number of people who are sufficiently knowledgeable about small business to be able to consider it rationally as a career alternative. There has been a sharp increase in this form of business education in both Europe and the United States, increasing attention being paid to under-graduates (Rosa 1989) and specific groups such as ethnic minorities (Mitra and Sarabjeet 1989) and women. More recently, secondary education programmes designed to increase awareness of industry have also become more sensitive to the small firm (Curran and Stanworth 1989:17). Of some interest is the fact that these writers emphasize the role played by the mass media in the UK in promoting the small business 'message' during the 1980s, reaching a wider audience than conventional educational avenues. At the same time, however, they are also cautious about the worrying tendency for media accounts to be superficial and over-optimistic in their portrayal of small business.

This review indicates that despite some innovative areas of potential development, small business education remains con-strained within fairly narrow limits. Indeed, these limits them-selves reflect the overall thrust of central government small business policy, namely that small business is unconditionally beneficial and to be encouraged at any cost (hence the prolifera-tion of courses concerned with a general business start-up theme and the rapid expansion of 'enterprise awareness' initiatives). Unfortunately, whilst these areas are politically fashionable, there is no reliable evidence to suggest that they are necessarily the most effective form of small business education. It could be the case, for example, that resources would be better used, both in terms of creating jobs and viable businesses, if education was concentrated upon already functioning businesses rather than upon the multitude of potential start-up ideas that may have little chance of anything other than the most short-term survival. It is something of an irony that the criterion of 'relevance' so keenly applied to other (politically unfashionable) areas of education identified by the government as 'unproductive' has conveniently ignored small business education.

Whatever the reasons for this lack of research, an assessment of the most effective teaching strategies and evaluation of results measured by the numbers of successful small business brought into being and their progress over time should be a major area for future work. Without it, policy and resource utilisation in small business education will remain largely guesswork, at the mercy of political fashions.
(Curran and Stanworth 1989:20)

In addition to formal education and training, however, an alternative source of advice and information for small businesses has been provided by Local Enterprise Agencies (LEAs). These usually take the form of a 'company limited by guarantee' and, as such, are formally independent of central government, although the latter has lent considerable moral and ideological support to such ventures. Thus, according to Engellau (1984:8), the 1980s have seen the establishment of a whole network of independent bodies giving free advice to small-scale businesses. These enterprise agencies are non-profit-making 'partnerships' jointly sponsored by local businesses and local authorities, intended to help small firms. The sponsors provide capital either in cash or in kind, the latter usually in the form of premises, equipment or seconded personnel who remain on the payroll of the seconding company.

In the late 1980s there were in excess of 400 LEAs in existence, providing a range of services from business information and counselling to business training, managed workspace, loan funding and small business clubs (Grayson 1989:534). These agencies are sponsored by over 5,000 companies, as well as by local authorities, and receive core funding from the Training Agency if part of an inner-city project scheme. For sponsors, tax relief is available on donations to enterprise agencies. Over 300 of these enterprise agencies are co-ordinated more or less closely by an umbrella organization, Business In the Community (BIC), established in 1981 with objectives to

- encourage industry and commerce to become more involved on a local basis with the economic, training, social and environmental needs of communities in which they operate;
- bring together local authorities, organisations and business to assist in the development of effective action;
- collect and disseminate information about successful local initiatives so that others can learn rapidly and effectively, and
- work through and support existing initiatives and organisations.

(Gibb and Durowse 1987:6)

Although the language of BIC and LEAs is couched in terms of a partnership between local government and big business, there would seem to be little doubt that the latter unambiguously takes the role of senior partner, setting the agenda and determining criteria of success and failure. Indeed, this should not be surprising as, contrary to recent idealized strands of government rhetoric, businesses are not charities, and generally expect to see some sort of return on their investment in LEAs. Such returns, of course, do not need to be immediate, nor do they have to be of a direct financial kind, although this may be the case in some instances. There are also indirect and longer-term pay-offs such as local 'goodwill', public relations, and, most long-term and indirect of all, safeguarding the stability of the capitalist system by helping to mitigate some of the harsher realities of an unrestrained market.

In terms of direct benefits, large businesses may view support for local enterprise as a means of facilitating their own rationalization plans, allowing them to subcontract previously internal services to external providers, frequently small businesses, and to 'slim down' staffing levels at the same time as appearing to provide alternative employment opportunities. As critics of such policies have pointed out, however, there is little guarantee that the number of new jobs created by local small business will be capable of matching the number of jobs lost by large organizations, and certainly not in the medium or short term, nor that the terms and conditions attached to the jobs created by new small firms will be comparable to those found in large organizations (Storey 1982; Rainnie 1989).

Big business support for LEAs may also result in the less direct, but none the less important, benefits of good public relations, both in relation to the wider 'community' and an organization's own workforce, particularly where corporate policies might otherwise be seen as socially damaging. For example, where plant closure would have a drastic, and politically undesirable, effect upon a local community, support for an LEA can show some evidence of the 'human face' of the corporation. It can also, of course, set a convenient precedent if that company envisages that it will have to take the same kind of action in other problem sites in future, and therefore wishes to have a procedure which will be accepted by unions and the local community (Gibb and Durowse 1987:5).

An even longer-term view of the benefits available to big business in assisting local small business initiatives is to be found within organizations such as Shell and IBM. Gibb and Durowse quote IBM's Director of Personnel and Corporate Affairs thus:

We view the fulfilment of our corporate responsibilities as an essential investment helping to maintain the society in which a business can flourish .... Such activities are not seen by IBM as either a drain, or an alternative to, profit. The company's view is that the long-term profit-making potential and continued survival of industry will be jeopardised unless companies invest in the community.
(Gibb and Durowse 1987:5)

Overall, then, there can be little doubt that small business policy has been a growth area in the 1980s, and in a manner which, almost uniquely, has spanned central and local government and the public and private sectors. What is less certain, however, is the effectiveness of these policies. Already questions have emerged concerning the monitoring and control of such measures and the apparent disregard of evidence that fails to fit the 'small is beautiful' caricature. In this respect, Gibb and Durowse's account of the evaluation of big business assistance to LEAs is indicative of the problems encountered in most other areas of small business policy analysis. Regarding LEAs, for instance, they point to the present impossibility of measuring either inputs to or outputs from these organizations, either in terms of actions taken, or of resulting jobs and profits. Their assessment is worthy of lengthy quotation:

A ... questionnaire survey carried out independently in February 1985 covered 148 agencies .... This asked questions about resources consumed as well as outputs. The replies from 134 agencies indicated that their support totalled £14.8 million in cash or in kind – an average of £111,000 per agency each year. About three-quarters of this was cash income. These agencies were receiving support from 1,491 sponsoring companies, organisations or individuals, and there were, on average, 18 sponsors per agency. The 'outputs' of the agencies were slightly more optimistic than those obtained by [an] ... 'in-house' survey, indicating that, in total, an average 286 new jobs were associated with enterprise agency activity in a year, along with 130 jobs saved. These results, however, must be treated with reserve. Numerous studies demonstrate how difficult it is to associate limited inputs of advice or assistance to the 'out-puts' of companies or individuals receiving the assistance. There are a wide variety of factors involved in determining ultimate success, and in-puts of training or counselling usually constitute a very small part .... Sadly, there is almost no evidence of the impact of large companies on

Small business and society

changing attitudes towards entrepreneurship or small business in local communities.

(Gibb and Durowse 1987:14)

The one factor which unites the numerous and diverse range of small business policy initiatives introduced by the Thatcher administration would seem, inescapably, to be the priority of political preference (some might say prejudice) over reasoned argument and empirically substantiated investigation. Thus, despite the claims that small business policy helps to create jobs and stimulate entrepreneurship, there is very little conclusive evidence to suggest that it has produced real 'additionality' (events that would not have taken place without the policy intervention), except in the negative sense of removing legislative protection from workers.

In the policy field, then, it seems that small business leads a charmed life. This, in no small part, is attributable to political fashion, but social scientists have also played their part by allowing free-passage to the notion that small business can be understood as an homogeneous category, thereby doing very little to hinder the propagation of gross over-simplifications and unsustainable generalizations. It is this point that provides the theme for the concluding chapter.

Chapter eight

Conclusions

If there is a single conclusion which arises from this book it must be the exposure of the folly of treating small business as a homogeneous category. The diversity of activity and organization revealed in the foregoing chapters makes it abundantly clear that a genuine understanding of small business cannot be premised upon the assumption of commonality amongst enterprises below a specified size threshold, nor upon the existence of a unified 'small firm sector'. Whilst such assumptions and labels are convenient for statistical and rhetorical purposes, their qualitative validity is open to severe question.

There are four areas in which the assumption of small business homogeneity can lead to profound inadequacies of understanding. These inadequacies will be referred to as 'homogenization effects'. The first of these is the encouragement of a tendency towards essentialism: that is to say, the attribution to small businesses in general of some fundamental and ontologically privileged quality, e.g., 'entrepreneurship', 'industrial harmony', 'innovation', etc.

Second, the assumption of homogeneity implies the existence of common small business interests and a shared outlook amongst their owners and workers.

Third, it creates problems of definition and conceptualization, particularly in terms of the nature of small business organizational structure.

Finally, the assumption of a unitary small business sector discourages the examination of small firms in their wider economic and social context – i.e., it implies that small business exhibits its own distinct dynamic relatively independently of extraneous relations.

As the reader should now be aware, none of these positions can rigorously be sustained in the light of the analysis presented in the previous pages. To consolidate this view, each area will be subject to summary analysis in the light of the data and ideas so far discussed.

The limitations of small business essentialism were made readily apparent by the discussion of free-market, Marxian, and Green approaches in Chapter one. The first of these, the free-market perspective, posited a model of small business premised upon a fundamental entrepreneurialism. As, it argued, entrepreneurship is the dynamo of market society, and as its most readily available expression is in the formation of small businesses, such businesses must play a key role in the economic rejuvenation of capitalist society. Indeed, this argument is extended to suggest that the reason for the post-war slump in the UK's fortunes is largely attributable to the decline of the small business sector at the expense of monopolies and big government. In this way the assumed essential characteristic of entrepreneurship serves as a basis for elevating small business to a theoretically privileged position as a causal agent in the economic process. This, in turn, is supported by a normative model of small business which draws upon the supposed social and psychological dimensions of entrepreneurship to bolster the political ideology of the Enterprise Culture and Popular Capitalism. The empirical support for these 'essential' assumptions, however, is severely limited and, upon careful scrutiny, the free-market conception of small business appears as little more than a romanticized chimera that systematic-ally distorts or marginalizes that which is inconsistent with the ideology of Enterprise. Thus, this approach has supported the view that employment relations in small firms are essentially harmonious and consensual, a view shown in Chapter four to be a profound oversimplification. Similarly, it has encouraged the notion that small businesses are inherently innovatory and, as such, are in the vanguard of reindustrialization through high technology. Again, this was shown in Chapter six to be both a muddled and misleading account of small business activity. Finally, in Chapter seven it was shown that this uncritical faith in the economic and social potency of small business has encouraged a rash of policy initiatives to encourage and support small firms with only minimal concern for their overall benefit to the community.

The Marxian and Green approaches, whilst having played a lesser role in affecting the practical fortunes of small business, fare little better than the free marketeers in terms of their theoretical assumptions. Within the former, for instance, the essential character of the small firm is not its economic primacy but, rather, its dependence upon the structure and strategies of large capital. The corollary of this position is to view small business as the object of a functional exploitation in the sphere of circulation (i.e., as a result of the market dominance of large capital), which is reflected in the small firm's division of labour as 'hyper-exploitation'. According to this view small business has little to offer society in general. The only real beneficiary of a thriving small business sector is the capitalist class; even small business owners and the self-employed may find themselves the victims of this restructuring of capital as they are driven out of business or their profits squeezed in line with the short-term exigencies of big business. And this, of course, says nothing of the low wages, dangerous conditions, and lack of trade union protection supposedly suffered by workers in small firms. If this position is accepted then there can be no justification for the use of public funds to stimulate and support small business growth. Empirical support for this view, however, is equally limited, certainly in terms of establishing the functional dependence of small business generally, and in relation to any inherent tendency for small firms to be 'hyper-exploiters' of labour. It is one thing to say that the health of small business is dependent upon the overall health of the economy and that this, in turn, is conditioned largely by the activities of large capital. But it is quite another thing to imply that this dependence is a necessary and functional adjunct of capitalist strategy rather than a contingent feature of particular industries. Thus, it is quite possible to recognize that large firms do utilize subcontracting relations to exploit small firms, without simultaneously taking on board the notions either that this is a condition of existence for all small businesses, or that it necessarily leads to the hyper-exploitation of labour. The latter is a possibility but it is by no means a certainty.

The essentialism of the Green approach is primarily moral. It stems from the belief that there is something inherently humane in small-scale organization, either in its potential for democratic participation or, less specifically, as a vehicle for the non-violent satisfaction of material and spiritual needs. Whilst this may have a certain intuitive appeal (and a long intellectual pedigree in one form or another), it is distinctly difficult to sustain when applied to what is known about small-scale organizations as they exist *now* . In short, the essential humanity of small-scale organization seems to be derived not from empirical investigation but from meta-physical speculation: that is, what such organizations might become rather than what they are. This, of course, is especially problematic for the analysis of small business, since it involves, on the one hand, ignoring the reality of exploitation and degradation that can be associated with small firms and, on the other hand, romanticizing the prospects for the establishment of 'alternative' forms of small business. As Chapter five revealed, co-operatives, the form of small business most favoured by the Green approach, appear to enjoy an even less stable existence in advanced industrial economies than conventional small firms. Also, as was seen in Chapter seven, small-scale organization alone seems to do little to prevent industrial injury or unfair treatment of workers. In this light it can be seen that the Green slogan 'small is beautiful' is a tenet of faith which, however laudable, has little to recommend it as the starting point for a satisfactory analysis of the 'real world' of small business.

The second category of 'homogenization effects' is associated with the assumption of common small business interests and shared outlook amongst owners and workers. Whilst such assumptions are a natural corollary of small business essentialism of the kind just discussed, they can also be found in work that claims to be empirically rather than theoretically informed. Chapter three, for instance, provided many illustrations of attempts to establish common characteristics of small business owners along dimensions varying from personality traits and childhood experiences to political orientations. Most of these have foundered by trying to generalize their findings from small and unrepresentative samples to small business owners in general. As the volume of empirical research in this area grows, revealing increasing diversity, the inadequacy of such attempts becomes readily apparent. Such projects, however, are not the simple consequence of method-ological laxity. They, too, reflect the prior assumption (albeit not necessarily theoretically derived) that it is meaningful to speak of small business as a generic category. As Chapters two and three demonstrated, such an assumption, of course, cannot now be sustained. It certainly cannot be used as the basis for deducing common interests. Unfortunately, the widespread use of an arbitrary size threshold (e.g., below 200 employees) as the defining characteristic of small business suggests a unity that is, in reality, spurious. Size alone is not a structural variable and, as such, cannot be expected to highlight that network of divisions that will fragment any given small business population thus defined. Such divisions will be associated, most obviously, with inter- and intra-industrial sector differences, but will also follow lines of class, gender and ethnicity. Indeed, there is no a priori reason to suppose that, in itself, the size of a business will have any particular influence on the interests and outlook of a proprietor such as to override that generated by other social identities the individual may hold. Thus, the self-employed and small employers in Scase and Goffee's study of the building trade identified their interests as those of craft workers (Scase and Goffee 1982); whilst the radical proprietors in their later work on female business owners defined their interests in terms of feminism (Goffee and Scase 1985). Indeed, these writers and others have developed empirically based typologies of small business owners that emphasize the variety of proprietorial interests and outlook rather than their unity. The point is not that small business owners do not have common interests, but that these are as likely to arise from specific situational needs as from any universal property of size. As Parr has remarked in a guide to organizations claiming to represent small firms:

> Although stated frequently enough, the implications rarely seem to be thoroughly comprehended; there is no 'typical' small firm. Thus, the needs and objectives of small firms and businesses ... are literally multi-variate. This is related not only to the individual characteristics of the proprietors and the type of operation being carried on but also, and possibly more significantly, to the dynamics of the particular firm, i.e. whether it is growth oriented, marking time or whether it is in an industry which is in temporary or long-term decline.
> (Parr 1983:1)

Similar points can be made in relation to workers in small firms. Chapter four revealed the variety of forms which employment relations in small firms may take, ranging from fraternalism to sweated labour, and how these reflected particular balances of power within the workplace and labour market. There was virtually no support for the conventional wisdom that small-scale organization leads inevitably to industrial harmony and to high levels of attachment between employer and employed. Whilst size undoubtedly plays a part in structuring the pattern of harmonious working relations, this is no reason to suppose that it brings about the existence of such harmony in the first place. In the cases studied this could either be explained by other variables (e.g., employers' dependence on skilled labour in a tight labour market, or the effect of industrial subculture), or opened to question on the grounds of superficiality (i.e., the appearance of harmony resulting from pragmatic acquiescence rather than moral attachment).

The third 'homogenization effect' concerns the definition and conceptualization of small business. The use of arbitrary statistical definitions stipulating a maximum size threshold above which a business cannot be considered 'small' has certainly contributed to the lack of attention paid to the organizational structure of small firms. Thus, although it has commonly been pointed out that, even to the casual observer, there is a clear difference between, say, the self-employed artisan, the small employer with a handful of workers, and the family firm with perhaps 200 employees, relatively little has been done to distinguish these (and other forms of small business) conceptually. Indeed, as far as an arbitrary statistical definition is concerned, there is no difference: any organization with fewer than (usually) 200 workers *is* a small firm. The move away from such definitions, however, has been slow, although progress does now seem to be being made (e.g., Curran and Burrows 1989). Scase and Goffee (1982), for example, introduced a four-fold typology of small businesses differentiated according to proprietorial function and the relative mix of labour and capital utilized. They distinguished between the self-employed, small employers, owner-controllers, and owner-directors (see Chapter one of this book), in ascending order of organizational complexity and sophistication. In their initial work on this subject Scase and Goffee suggested that these qualitative types of small business would be roughly related to size and level of business activity, although their own data were not able to demonstrate this conclusively. Later research by Hakim using a nationally representative data-base appears to have gone some way towards validating this assertion. Her research identifies 'key watersheds' in business expansion (measured by the number of employees), each of which 'marks a qualitative change in the nature of the business rather than just a small addition to the size of the workforce' (Hakim 1989:37). Hakim's data (discussed in Chapter two of this book) relates primarily to small businesses with fewer than fifty workers, where the 'break-points' appear as follows:

- 1 to 2 workers: the self-employed person with at most one other full-time worker/partner;
- 3 to 9 full-time employees;
- 10 to 24 full-time employees;
- 25 to 49 full-time employees.

She does suggest, however, that there may be another significant break-point at 100 employees. Clearly these results do not allow the direct transposition of size bands into the Scase and Goffee typology, neither should this be expected, since the precise physical size at which a qualitative change in organizational form occurs will be affected by the nature of the industrial sector under study, the managerial abilities and aspirations of the proprietor, and the development of the technical and social division of labour. Thus the exact configuration of break-points might be expected to vary between industrial sectors, one category being subsumed within another depending upon conditions. Nevertheless, what these data do do is to confirm the existence of qualitative distinctions in small business organizational structure in a statistically reliable manner, and to further weaken the grounds for the continued use of arbitrary size definitions as anything other than an initial screening device.

These points have received yet more support from the investigations of Curran and Burrows (1988;1989) and Hakim (1988; 1989b) into the nature of self-employment and the distinctions between this form of business and other types of small firm. Indeed, Hakim (1988:445) goes so far as to argue for the necessity of a reasonably reliable conceptual framework to distinguish different types of self-employed businesses. Clearly, much work remains to be done in this area, but there are at least the beginnings of attempts to undermine the 'homogenizing effect' of restricted and arbitrary definitions.

Finally, there remain to be considered those 'homogenization effects' which isolate small businesses from their wider economic and social context, encouraging an inward-looking and narrow analysis. These are associated with, in particular, a reliance upon the notion of a 'small firm sector' and the implication that this can be studied in its own right as an autonomous site of industrial activity. Here again, the empirical distortion which such an approach involves – in effect the decontextualization of small business – has been widely recognized but little attended to. These distortions can include the blurring of inter-industrial (and intra-sectoral) differences and, more importantly, the obscuring of the relationship between small businesses and other forms of economic activity. In this area Marxian approaches have provided the most consistent challenge to the latter effect, albeit somewhat blunted by the tendency towards essentialism noted above. The most developed of these has been that employed by Rainnie (1989) to map out the patterns and degrees of dependency between large and small firms, using the categories of dependent, competitive independent, old independent, and new independent small businesses. Each category attempts to delineate not only the type of small business activity involved but also the ways in which this is actually or potentially linked to the fortunes of big business (see Chapter one).

A non-Marxist contribution to this area of debate is provided by Hakim (1988), who uses a labour market model (Loveridge 1983) to analyse the relationship between the growth in self-employment and employers' subcontracting strategies. Similarly, the approach of 'community dynamics' developed by Shearman and Burrell

(1988) provides another attempt to link small businesses to their wider economic environment (see Chapter five of this book). A related perspective is utilized by Pyke (1988), who draws attention to networks of co-operation between small and medium-sized manufacturing establishments which emerge frequently as a means of coping with the influence of large and powerful buying organizations (e.g., retail chains). Depending on the intensity of such influences, Pyke identifies four types of co-operative network: trusting co-operation, forced co-operation, dependent co-operation, and specialist independent co-operation. Small business, therefore, does not exist in an economic and social 'vacuum', and whilst there may be certain very general contexts in which it is appropriate to speak of a small firm sector, it is clearly dangerous to treat this as an empirical fact rather than a convenient generalization.

To limit these 'homogenizing effects' is clearly a necessity if a restricted, 'one-dimensional' view of the small firm is to be avoided. The alternative suggested by this book is the development of a sociological approach that encourages the use of empirically open-ended concepts capable of capturing and elucidating the diversity of small business activity. Much clearly remains to be done in this respect, but it does now seem that after a decade of hectic small business research the basis has been laid for the development of a critical understanding of small business, not merely in its own terms, but in its wider social context. It is hoped that this book will stimulate others to develop such an approach more fully.

Notes

Chapter One   Theories of small business and society

1 Critics have suggested that the Government's treatment of the public sector reveals the application of the 'small-firm model' of industrial relations – either by the imposition of 'competitive tendering', the introduction of decentralized 'profit centres', and the encouragement of individualized performance/profit-related pay schemes – in an attempt to break the power of public-sector unions.

2 This is not strictly accurate because both Poulantzas and Wright do conceive the petty bourgeoisie not as a product of capitalist relations of production but an earlier, more primitive mode: simple commodity production. As such it exists 'alongside' the classes thrown up by capitalist relations rather than 'between' them.

Chapter Two   The empirical investigation of UK small businesses

1 As examples of moves in this direction they give qualified support to the work of Rainnie (1989, see Chapter One of this book), Scase and Goffee (1982), Goffee and Scase (1985) and Stanworth and Curran (1986).

2 These figures, derived from OECD sources (see Hakim 1989b) include self-employed individuals who also employ labour, although most of the growth has consisted of one-person businesses without employees.

3 Put crudely, the Type 'A' personality shows strong tendencies towards competitiveness, achievement, aggression, tension and unpredictability; Type 'B' personalities, on the other hand, tend to be more relaxed, guilt-free, less prone to anger and aggression, and with a lower need to display achievement (Friedman and Rosenman 1974).

4 Particular confusion has been caused by the terms 'net' and 'gross' new jobs which are central to an accurate interpretation of Birch's results, and to most subsequent studies by other researchers. This distinction is captured diagrammatically by Storey (1982), as shown in Figure 2.1n, who summarizes Birch's findings as follows:

1 Gross job loss through contraction and closure was about 8 per cent per annum.

2 In 'replacing' these jobs, (i.e., gross job gains) about 50 per cent were created through expansions of existing companies and about 50 per cent through new openings.

3 About 50 per cent of gross jobs created by openings were produced by independent, free-standing entrepreneurs (births) and 50 per cent by multi-plant operations (in moves).

4 Firms employing less than twenty people generated 66 per cent of net new jobs in the United States.

Presenting Birch's findings in this way makes clear that to claim that small firms create 66 per cent of net jobs is not the same as saying they create 66 per cent of *all* jobs, or 66 per cent of gross jobs, as has often been claimed. Indeed, subsequent studies in both the USA and elsewhere have been less optimistic in assessing the job generation potential of small business.

Figure 2.1n The job generation process

births			
+	=	openings	
in moves		+	= *gross new jobs*
		expansions	(replacement jobs)
			(gross job gains)
		contractions	= *net job*
out moves		+	change
+		closures	= gross job losses	(total net
deaths			jobs) (net
			new jobs)

(terms in brackets are synonyms for unbracketed terms)

Source: Storey (1982)

5 Despite the useful and wide-ranging data which this survey supplies, however, it is not truly representative of small business in Britain, a fact recognized by its producers who highlight its limitations (Table 2.1n).

Table 2.1n Representative characteristics of *Quarterly Survey* sample

Characteristics of business	Under-represented	Over-represented
Legal status	Sole proprietor	Limited company
Sector of trade	Agriculture, forestry and fisheries	Manufacturing, distributive trades and other services
Region	Midlands (East & West), South-East, Wales	Scotland, South-West, East Anglia
Turnover	£50,000 and below	
Employment	1–9 employees	10–100+ employees
Age of business	Younger firms (5 yrs & under)	Older firms (6 yrs +)

Source: SBRT (1989) 4, 4:12

6 Performance in terms of turnover and employment can be seen in Table 2.7, measured by a summary statistic – the 'balance' – which represents the percentage of respondents replying 'up' minus the percentage replying 'down'.

Chapter Three Small business and the entrepreneur

1 McClelland regards entrepreneurs as exhibiting the following characteristics: a liking for moderate risk-taking; confidence in one's ability to succeed; energetic action directed towards self-advancement; the desire for freedom and individual responsibility; individual success, usually measured by the acquisition of wealth. All these characteristics are held to be strongly associated with achievement motivation.
2 McClelland limited his attention to male children, which is perhaps not surprising given that only very recently has female entrepreneurship been considered worthy of serious attention by academics and commentators.
3 Loosely following Goffee and Scase (1985), 'managerial orientation' is defined as a combination of knowledge of and competence in basic managerial functions, an endorsement of the market as an arbiter of individual success, and a more or less developed sense of long- to medium-term business goals and objectives. 'Vocational attachment' refers to the extent to which an individual is committed to a particular form of industrial activity as an end in itself. Thus, a high level of vocational attachment will imply that work is a source of intrinsic satisfaction and the pursuance of vocational goals a source of self-expression and identity. A low level of vocational attachment will imply an instrumental approach to work – as a means to an end rather than an end in itself. Four proprietorial types can be described using these dimensions – Figure 3.1n.

Figure 3.1n Dimensions of occupational role and managerial style

Managerial orientation			
		High	*Low*
Vocational Attachment	High	(2) Technocentric	(1) Traditional
	Low	(3) Marketeering	(4) Isolationist

Source: Goss (1989:104)

4 These authors are careful to point out that the relationship between entrepreneurial identity and growth is not a simple evolutionary one which is in some sense fixed by immutable personality traits, but rather it is dynamic, changeable and, above all, responsive to changes in social situation. In other words, the very success of an initial entrepreneurial role may lead to a reassessment of that role and its implications, which,

in turn, stimulates the individual to change direction and perhaps take on a new role to cope with the changed circumstances. For example, the successful acting out of the managerial role may lead to a situation where the entrepreneur feels he or she has done no more than create the sort of bureaucratized organization from which he or she was trying to escape as an employee.

Chapter Four   Employment relations in small firms

1 Here may also be found the rhetoric of paternalism but without the substantive elements which constitute the sociologically distinct concept developed by Newby. Goffee and Scase (1985), for instance, use the label of 'maternalism' to describe a strategy employed by the 'conventional' businesswomen which they regard as a parallel to paternalism. On close inspection, however, it is apparent that this strategy is qualitatively distinct from paternalism, either as described by Newby or Goffee and Scase in their earlier work (1982). They describe maternalism thus:

> A key assumption underlying the maternalist strategy is that employers use their authority to act benignly in the interests of employees. Thus, the *arbitrary* decision-making of proprietors is perceived to be quite legitimate by employees since it is assumed that the outcomes will be to their advantage. In return for this benevolence, employees are expected to show commitment, loyalty and gratitude.
> (Goffee and Scasse 1985:89; emphasis added)

What seems to be missing from maternalism which justifies the claim of its being analogous to paternalism is the notion of mutual duties and obligations which go beyond the simple desire to treat employees 'fairly' or benignly (Goffee and Scase 1982). Additionally, Goffee and Scase (1985) make frequent references to the arbitrary decision-making power of maternalistic employers. Arbitrariness, however, is not a component of paternalistic authority, where, in fact, great emphasis is placed upon the fact that the decisions of superiors are based not upon personal whim or arbitrary demands but are taken in line with the established authority of tradition (Newby 1977; Weber 1978). Indeed, such arbitrary decision-making, particularly if in response to market forces alone, was shown to be a factor leading to the undermining of paternalism (Lane and Roberts 1971; Martin and Fryer 1973).

2 These data are taken from a larger study of thirty-nine small firms in the general printing industry in South-East England conducted between 1984 and 1986 (Goss 1986). In each case the proprietor of the firm was interviewed, as were some employees in a number of firms. The semi-structured interviews were tape-recorded and later transcribed in full. All the full interview transcripts were subjected to a careful content-analysis and were referenced according to salient topics. These references were used to check for consistency and diversity, both

within individual interviews and between respondents and groups of respondents. Except where a divergence of response is indicated, the quotations used as illustrations can be considered typical of the relevant responses within the particular group under discussion. The sample was selected in a non-random fashion.

3 For example, as (then) Employment Minister Peter Morrison said of the YOP: 'The scheme is not a social service. Its purpose is to teach youngsters what the real world of work is all about.' However, as Finn remarked, 'The MSC takes for granted the demands of employers and seeks to adjust the supply of labour accordingly' (Finn 1983). For further details see Goss (1987).

4 The following data are derived from seven colour printing firms ranging in size from four to thirty-two workers. (See note 4.2.)

Chapter Five   Alternative forms of small business

1 The fifth and sixth types, the Small Business Man and the Skilled Escapee, are not considered here as they represent forms of entrepreneurial activity that are primarily legal (Hobbs 1988:169ff)

Chapter Six   Small business, new technology and innovation

1 The critique of Rothwell and Oakey provided by Shearman and Burrell is strongly rejected by both the former writers, who regard it as a distortion of their views and a misrepresentation of their research results (see Rothwell and Oakey [1989] *New Technology, Work and Employment* 4, 2, for the detailed responses provoked by Shearman and Burrell). In particular they reject the claim that they have been uncritical and unqualified proponents of small business in a way which reflects political partisanship.

2 Rainnie arrives at a similar conclusion where he draws attention to the dominance of large organizations in the electronics industry and, in consequence, the ultimately limited and dependent role of smaller enterprises, both in terms of producing totally novel innovations and in terms of job generation potential (Rainnie 1989:145ff).

3 Although the present focus is upon micro-processor-based technological change this should not be taken to imply that this is the only form of new technology with implications for small business. There are other fields of new technology – e.g., biotechnology and medical lasers (Shearman and Burrell 1988) – that have developed almost entirely independently of developments in the field of electronics. As yet, however, there is relatively little research material available for these areas (see e.g., Bollard 1983).

4 This division predates Braverman's intervention (1974), although this gave it wider currency amongst industrial sociologists, having its principal origins in the debate on the 'post-industrial society' popularized by Bell (1967), which focused upon the question of whether technological development was benign or malignant (see, for example, Douglas [1971]).

Chapter Seven   Small business policy

1 According to Hakim,

> The results only report probabilistic statements, without denying that the opposite can also be true, albeit less commonly so. For example, three-quarters of fast-growth firms have separate business premises, but then so to do roughly half of no-growth firms. Two-thirds of the no-growth firms employ only one to two people, but then this is also true of one-quarter of fast-growth firms. Almost half of the fast-growth firms are limited companies, but then again so are one fifth of the no-growth businesses. And so on. None of the characteristics of no-growth and fast-growth firms are mutually exclusive to a sufficient degree to allow us to make predictions about future expansion. (Hakim 1989a:38)

2 Unfortunately the report gives no details of sample size or coverage, etc.

References

Aldrich, H. and Stern, R. (1983) 'Resource mobilisation and the creation of US producer's co-operatives', *Economic and Industrial Democracy* 4, 3: 371–406.

Aldrich, H., Jones, T., Zimmer, C. (1986) 'Small business still speaks with the same voice: a replication of "the voice of small business and the politics of survival"', *Sociological Review* 34, 2: 335–56.

Allen, D. (1987) *Enterprise Allowance Scheme Evaluation*, Sheffield: Manpower Services Commission.

Anthony, P. (1977) *The Ideology of Work*, London: Tavistock.

Argyle, M. and Little, B. (1972) 'Do personality traits apply to social behaviour?', *Journal for the Theory of Social Behaviour* 2, 1: 1–35.

Austin, T. (1980) 'The "lump" in the UK construction industry', in T. Nichols (ed) *Capital and Labour*, London: Fontana.

Bannock, G. (1981) *The Economics of Small Firms*, Oxford: Basil Blackwell.

Beaumont, P. and Rennie, I. (1986) 'Organisational culture and non-union status of small businesses', *Industrial Relations Journal* 19, 2: 214–24.

Bechhofer, F., Bland, R., Elliott, B. and Rushforth, M. (1974) 'Small shopkeepers: matters of money and meaning', *Sociological Review* 22: 465–82.

Beesley, M. and Wilson, P. (1981) 'Government aid to small firms in Britain', in P. Gorb, P. Dowell and P. Wilson (eds) *Small Business Perspectives*, London: Armstrong.

Bell, D. (1967) *The Coming of Post-Industrial Society*, New York: Basic Books.

Birch, D. (1979) *The Job Generation Process*, Cambridge, Mass.: MIT.

Blackburn, R. and Curran, J. (1989) 'The future of the small firm: attitudes of young people to entrepreneurship', paper presented to the 12th UK Small Firms Policy and Research Conference, Thames Polytechnic, London, November.

Blackburn, R. and Hankinson, A. (1989) 'Training in the smaller business', *Industrial and Commercial Training* 21: 27–9.

Blau, P., Falbe, C., McKinley, W. and Tracy, P. (1976) 'Technology and organisation in manufacturing', *Administrative Science Quarterly* 21: 20–40.

References

Bollard, A. (1983) 'Technology, economic change and small firms', *Lloyds Bank Review* 147.

Bolton Report (1971) *Committee of Inquiry on Small Firms*, London: HMSO, Cmnd 4811.

Boswell, J. (1973) *The Rise and Decline of Small Firms*, London: George Allen and Unwin.

Braverman, H. (1974) *Labour and Monopoly Capital*, New York, Monthly Review Press.

Brenson, M., Wray, K., Bryman, A., Beardsworth, A., Ford, J. and Keil, E. (1985) 'The flexibility of recruitment in the construction industry', *Sociology* 19, 1: 108–24.

Burns, T. and Stalker, G. (1961) *The Management of Innovation*, London: Tavistock.

Burrows, R. (1991) (ed.) Deciphering the Enterprise Culture: Entrepreneurship, Petty capitalism and the Restructuring of Britain, London: Routledge.

Campbell, A. and Warner, M. (1987) 'New technology, innovation and training: an empirical study of selected British firms', *New Technology, Work and Employment* 2, 2: 86–100.

Carter, S. and Cannon, T. (1988) 'Women in business', *Employment Gazette*, October: 565–71.

Chell, E. (1986) 'The entrepreneurial personality: a review and some theoretical developments', in J. Curran (ed.) *The Survival of the Small Firm*, vol. II, Aldershot: Gower.

Child, J. (1967) *Industrial Relations in the British Printing Industry*, London: George Allen & Unwin.

Chinoy, E. (1955) *Automobile Workers and the American Dream*, Doubleday, New York.

Churchill, D. (1988) 'A buoyant business', *Financial Times*, 1.10.88.

Clark, J. (1988) 'New technology and industrial relations', *New Technology, Work and Employment* 3, 1: 5–17.

Clegg, S. and Dunkerley, D. (1980) *Class, Power and Organisation*, London: Routledge & Kegan Paul.

Cockburn, C. (1983) *Brothers*, London: Pluto.

Cornforth, C. (1986) 'Worker co-operatives: factors affecting their success and failure', in J. Curran (ed.) *The Survival of the Small Firm*, Aldershot: Gower.

Cornforth, C. (1988) 'Can entrepreneurship be institutionalised? The case of worker co-operatives', *International Small Business Journal* 6, 4: 10–19.

Coyne, J. and Binks, M. (1983) *The Birth of Enterprise*, London: Institute of Economic Affairs.

Cromie, S. (1987) 'Similarities and differences between women and men who choose business proprietorship', *International Journal of Small Business* 5, 3: 43–60.

Cromie, S. and Hayes, J. (1988) 'Towards a typology of female entrepreneurs', *Sociological Review* 36, 1: 87–113.

Cross, M. (1983) 'The United Kingdom', in D. Storey (ed.) *The Small Firm*, London: Croom Helm.

Curran, J. (1986) 'The survival of the petite bourgeoisie: production and reproduction', in J. Curran (ed.) *The Survival of the Small Firm*, vol. II, Aldershot: Gower.

Curran, J. (1987) *Small Enterprises and their Environments*, Kingston: Small Business Research Unit.

Curran, J. and Burrows, R. (1988) *Enterprise in Britain: A National Profile of Small Business Owners and the Self-employed*, London: Small Business Research Trust.

Curran, J. and Burrows, R. (1989) 'Shifting the focus: problems and approaches to studying the small enterprise in the services sector', paper presented at 12th UK Small Firms Policy and Research Conference, Thames Polytechnic, London.

Curran, J. and Stanworth, J. (1986) 'Small firms, large firms: theoretical and research strategies for the comparative analysis of small and large firms', in M. Scott (ed.) *Small Firms: Researching their Growth and Development*, Aldershot: Gower.

Curran, J. and Stanworth, J. (1989) 'Education and training for enterprise: some problems of classification, evaluation, policy and research', *International Small Business Journal*, 7, 2: 11–22.

Davis, H. and Scase, R. (1985) *Western Capitalism and State Socialism*, Oxford: Basil Blackwell.

Douglas, J. (ed.) (1971) *The Technological Threat*, Englewood Cliffs: Prentice Hall.

Drucker, P. (1985) *Innovation and Entrepreneurship*, London: Pan.

Edwards, C. (1989) 'Small firms and new technology: some preliminary findings', paper presented at the 12th UK Small Business Policy and Research Conference, Thames Polytechnic, London, November.

Edwards, P. and Scullion, G. (1983) *The Social Organisation of Industrial Conflict*, London.

Edwards, R. (1979) *Contested Terrain*, London: Heinemann.

Engellau, P. (1984) *Enterprise Agencies*, Stockholm: Aspen.

Fevre, R. (1987) 'Sub contracting an industrial development', paper presented at the B.S.A. Conference, Edinburgh University.

Finn, D. (1983) 'Britain's misspent youth', *Marxism Today* 28.

Forester, A. (1978) 'Asians in Business', *New Society*, 23 Feb.

Fox, A. (1974) *Beyond Contract*, London: Faber.

Freeman C. (1983) *Long Waves in the World Economy*, London: Butterworths.

Freeman, C. (1984) *The Role of Technical Change in National Economic Development*, Brighton: University of Sussex, Science Policy Research Unit.

Friedman, A. (1977) *Industry and Labour*, London: Macmillan.

Friedman, M. and Rosenman, R. (1974) *Type A Behaviour and Your Heart*, London: Wildwood House.

Gallagher, C. and Stewart, H. (1985) *Jobs and the Business Life-cycle*, Research Report 2, University of Newcastle-upon-Tyne.

Ganguly, P. and Bannock, G. (1985) *UK Small Business Statistics and International Comparisons*, London: Harper & Row.

References

Gershuny, J. and Pahl, R. (1980) 'Britain in the decade of the three economies', in C. Littler (ed.), *The Experience of Work*, Aldershot: Gower.

Gibb, A. and Durowse, H. (1987) 'Large business support for small enterprise development in the UK', *Leadership and Organisational Development Journal* 8, 1: 3–16.

Gill, J. (1989) 'Providing effective help for infant business in areas of high unemployment', *International Small Business Journal* 7, 1: 43–51.

Goffee, R. and Scase, R. (1982) 'Fraternalism and paternalism as employer strategies in small firms', in G. Day (ed) *Diversity and Decomposition in the Labour market*, Aldershot: Gower.

Goffee, R. and Scase, R. (1985) *Women in Charge*, London: George Allen & Unwin.

Goss, D. (1986) *The Social Structure of the Small Firm*, PhD thesis, University of Kent.

Goss, D. (1987) 'Capitalist control and new technology', *Capital and Class* 31.

Goss, D. (1988a) 'Social harmony and the small firm: a reappraisal', *Sociological Review* 36, 1: 114–32.

Goss, D. (1988b) 'Diversity, complexity and technological change: an empirical study of geneal printing', *Sociology* 22, 3: 417–31.

Goss, D. (1989) 'Management development and small business education: the implications of diversity', *Management Education and development* 20, 1: 100–11.

Grayson, D. (1989) 'At the roots of enterprise', *Employment Gazette*, October: 534–8.

Griffith, J. and Dorsman, M. (1986) 'SMEs, new technology and training', *International Small Business Journal*, 5, 3: 30–42.

Grossman, G. (1985) 'The second economy of the USSR' in C. Littler (ed.) *The Experience of Work*, Aldershot: Gower.

Gudgin, G. and Fothergill, S. (1979) 'Geographical variations in the rate of formation of new manufacturing firms', *Regional Studies* 18, 3: 200–6.

Hakim, C. (1988) 'Self-employment in Britain: recent trends and current issues', *Work, Employment and Society* 2, 4.

Hakim, C. (1989a) 'Identifying fast growth small firms', *Employment Gazette*, January.

Hakim, C. (1989b) 'New recruits to self-employment in the 1980s', *Employment Gazette*, June: 286–97.

Handy, C. (1978) *Understanding Organizations*, London: Harmondsworth.

Handy, C. (1984) *The Future of Work*, Oxford: Blackwell.

Harris, N. (1972) *Competition and the Corporate Society*, London: Methuen.

Hertz, L. (1987) *The Business Amazons*, New York: Andre Deutsch.

Hobbs, D. (1988) *Doing the Business: Entrepreneurship, the Working Class and Detectives in the East End of London*, Oxford: Oxford University Press.

Hodson, G. and Kaufman, R. (1982) 'Economic dualism', *American Sociological Review* 47.

Hoel, B. (1982) 'Contemporary clothing sweatshops' in J. West *Work, Women and the Labour Market*, London: Routledge & Kegan Paul.

Hornaday, J. and Aboud, J. (1971) 'Characteristics of successful entrepreneurs', *Personnel Psychologyy* 24: 141–53.

Hornaday, J. and Bunker, C. (1970) 'The nature of the entrepreneur', *Personnel Psychology*, 23: 45–54.

Hull, F. (1988) 'Inventions from R&D: organisational designs for efficient research performance', *Sociology* 22, 3: 393–415.

Ingham, G. (1967) 'Organisation size and orientation to work', *Sociology* 1, 3.

Ingham, G. (1970) *Size of Organisation and Worker Behaviour*, Cambridge: Cambridge University Press.

Irving, J. (1989) 'A factor of survival for small business', *Sunday Times*, 12 November, D17.

Jones, T. and McEvoy, D. (1986) 'Ethnic enterprise: the popular image', in J. Curran (ed.), *The Survival of the Small Firm*, vol. 1, Aldershot: Gower.

Keeble, D. and Kelly, T. (1986) 'New firms and high technology industry in the United Kingdom: the case of computer electronics', in D. Keeble and E. Wever (eds) *New Firms and Regional Development in Europe*, London: Croom Helm.

Kets de Vries, M. (1977) 'The entrepreneurial personality', *Journal of Management Studies*, February: 34–57.

Kirzner, I. (1979) *Perception, Opportunity and Profit*, Chicago: University of Chicago Press.

Knights, D. and Willmott, H. (1989) 'Power and subjectivity at work: from degradation to subjugation in social relations', *Sociology* 23, 4: 535–58.

Kondratiev, N. (1935) 'The long waves in economic life', *Review of Economic Statistics*, 17: 105–15.

Kreckel, R. (1980) 'Unequal opportunity structures and labour market segmentation', *Sociology* 14, 4.

Lambshead, C. and Levy, F. (1989) 'Stress and small business management', paper presented at 12th UK Small Business Policy and Research Conference, Thames Polytechnic, London, November.

Lane, T. and Roberts, K. (1971) *Strike at Pilkingtons*, London: Fontana.

Lee, D. (1981) 'Skill, craft and class', *Sociology* 15. 1.

Levidow, L. (1981) 'The social contract meets the twentieth century sweat shop', in L. Levidow, and T. Young, (eds) *Science, Technology and the Labour Process*, London: Conference of Socialist Economists.

Liles, P. (1981) 'Who are the entrepreneurs', in P. Gorb, P. Dowell and P. Wilson (eds) *Small Business Perspectives*, London: Armstrong.

Littler, C. and Salaman, G. (1982) 'Bravermania and beyond', *Sociology* 16, 2.

Littler, C. and Salaman, G. (1984) *Class at Work*, London: Batsford.

London and South East Regional Planning Conference (1987) *Growth of Small Business and Self Employment*, London: LSERPC.

Loveridge, R. (1983) 'Labour market segmentation and the firm' in J. Edwards, (ed) *Manpower Planning: Strategy and Techniques in an Organisational Context*, Chichester: John Wiley.

Lynn, R. (1969) 'Personality characteristics of a group of entrepreneurs', *Journal of Occupational Psychology* 43: 151–2.

McClelland, D. (1961) *The Achieving Society*, Princetown: Van Nostrand.

McRobbie, G. (1982) *Small is Possible*, London: Abacus.

Martin, R. and Fryer, R. (1973) *Redundancy and Paternalist Capitalism*, London.

Marx, K. and Engels, F. (1975) *Manifesto of the Communist Party*, Peking: Foreign Languages Press.

Mason, C. and Harrison, R. (1986) 'The regional impact of public policy towards small firms in the United Kingdon' in Keeble and Weaver (eds) *New Firms and Regional Development in Europe*, London: Croom Helm.

Mason, C. and Lloyd, P. (1985) 'Spatial variation in new firm formation' in D. Storey (ed) *Small Firms and Regional Development*, Cambridge: Cambridge University Press.

Maya, N. (1987) 'Small business and social mobility in France' in R. Scase and R. Goffee (eds) (1987).

Mischel, W. (1981) *Introduction to Personality*, New York: Holt, Rinehart & Winston.

Mitra, J. and Sarabjeet, S. (1989) 'Black/ethnic minority owned small firms and inner city regeneration', paper presented at 12th UK Small Business Policy and Research Conference, Thames Polytechnic, London, November.

Musson, A. (1954) *The Typographical Association*, Oxford: Oxford University Press.

Newby, H. (1977) *The Deferential Worker*, London: Penguin.

Nichols, T. (1986) 'Industrial injuries in British manufacturing in the 1980s', *Sociological Review*, 32, 2.

Nichols, T. (1988) 'On the analysis of size effects and accidents – a further comment', *Industrial Relations Journal* 19.

Oakey, R. (1984) *High Technology Small Firms*, London: Francis Pinter.

Owualah, S. (1988) 'Providing the necessary economic infrastructures for small businesses: whose responsibility?' *International Small Business Journal* 6, 1: 10–30.

Pahl, R. (1984) *Divisions of Labour*, Oxford: Basil Blackwell.

Parkin, F. (1979) *Marxism and Class Theory*, London: Tavistock.

Parr, R. (1983) *Which Voice? A Guide to Organisations Representing Small Firms*, Leicestershire Small Firms Centre.

Pearson, P.(1985) *Twilight Robbery*, London: Pluto.

Penn, R. (1983) 'Theories of skill and class structure', *Sociological Review*, 31.

Poulantzas, N. (1975) *Classes in Contemporary Capitalism*, London: Verso.

Poutsma, E. and Zwaard, A. (1988) 'Programming CNC equipment – the effects of automation in small industrial enterprises', *International Small Business Journal* 7, 2: 35–43.

Pyke, F. (1988) 'Co-operative practices among small and medium-sized establishments', *Work, Employment and Society* 2, 3: 352–365.

Rainnie, A. (1983) 'Industrial Relations in Small Firms', unpublished PhD thesis, Newcastle Polytechnic.

Rainnie, A. (1984) 'Combined and uneven development in the clothing industry', *Capital and Class* 22.

Rainnie, A. (1985) 'Small firms, big problems: the political economy of small business', *Capital and Class*, 25: 140–68.

Rainnie, A. (1989) *Industrial Relations in Small Firms*, London: Routledge.

Reich, M., Gordon, D. and Edwards, R. (1973) 'Dual labour markets', *American Economic Review*, 63.

Ridyard, D., Jones, I. and Foster, R. (1989) 'Economic evaluation of the loan guarantee scheme', *Employment Gazette*, August: 417–21.

Rosa, P. (1989) 'Family background and entrepreneurial activity in British graduates', paper presented at the 12th UK Small Business Policy and Research Conference, Thames Polytechnic, London, November.

Rose, R. (1983) *Getting by in Three Economies*, Strathclyde: Centre for the Study of Public Policy.

Rothwell, R. (1986) 'The role of small firms in technological innovation', in J. Curran (ed.) *The Survival of the Small Firm*, Aldershot: Gower.

Rothwell, R. and Zegveld, W. (1982) *Innovation and the Small and Medium Sized Firm*, London: Francis Pinter.

Saker, J. (1989) 'Competitive advantage in small ethnic minority businesses: a reappraisal of the role of social networks', paper presented at the 12th UK Small Business Policy and Research Conference, Thames Polytechnic, London, November.

Salaman G, (1986) *Working*, London: Tavistock.

Scase, R. (1982) 'The petty bourgeoisie and modern capitalism', in A. Giddens and G. Mackenzie, (eds) *Social Class and the Division of Labour*, Cambridge: Cambridge University Press.

Scase, R. and Goffee, R. (1980) *The Real World of the Small Business Owner*, London: Croom Helm.

Scase, R. and Goffee, R. (1981) 'Traditional petty bourgeois attitudes', *Sociological Review*, 29.

Scase, R. and Goffee, R. (1982) *The Entrepreneurial Middle Class*, London: Croom Helm.

Scase, R. and Goffee, R. (eds) (1987) *Entrepreneurship in Europe: Social Processes*, London: Croom Helm.

Schumacher, F. (1974) *Small is Beautiful*, London: Abacus.

Schumpeter, J. (1939) *Business Cycles: A Theoretical, Historical, and Statistical Analysis of the Capitalist Process*, New York: McGraw Hill.

Schutt, J. and Whittington, R. (1984) 'Large firms and the rise of small units', paper presented to Small Business Research Conference, Nottingham.

References

Scott, M. and Rainnie, A. (1982) 'Beyond Bolton – industrial relations in small firms', in J. Stanworth, (ed) *Perspectives on a Decade of Small Business Research: Bolton Ten Years On*, Aldershot: Gower.

Segal/Quince (1985) *The Cambridge Phenomenon*, Segal/Quince and Partners.

Shearman, C. and Burrell, G. (1987) 'The structures of industrial development', *Journal of Management Studies* 24, 4.

Shearman, C. and Burrell, G. (1988) 'New technology based firms and the emergence of new industries: some employment indications', *New Technology, Work and Employment* 3, 2: 87–99.

Small Business Research Trust (1984–9) *Quarterly Survey of Small Business in Britain*, London.

Solomon, T. and Fernald, L. (1988) 'Value profiles of male and female entrepreneurs', *International Small Business Journal* 6, 3: 24–33.

Stanworth, J. and Curran, J. (1978) 'Some reasons why small is not beautiful'; *New Society*, 14 December.

Stanworth, J. and Curran, J. (1979) 'Worker involvement and social relations in the small firm', *Sociological Review* 27.

Stanworth, J. and Curran, J. (1981) 'Size of workplace and attitudes to industrial relations', *British Journal of Industrial Relations* XIX: 14–25.

Stanworth, J. and Curran, J. (1982) 'Growth and the small firm', in P. Gorb, P. Dowell, and P. Wilson (eds) *Small Business Perspectives*, London: Armstrong.

Stanworth, J. and Curran, J. (1986) 'The franchised small enterprise: formal and operational dimensions of independence', in J. Lewis, J. Stanworth, and A. Gibb (eds) *Success and Failure in Small Business*, Aldershot: Gower.

Stephenson, G., Brotherton, G., Delafield, P. and Skinner, M. (1983) 'Size of organisation, attitudes to work and job satisfaction', *Industrial Relations Journal* 14: 141–63.

Stevens, M. (1988) 'Unfair dismissal cases in 1985–6, characteristics of the parties', *Employment Gazette*, December: 651–9.

Stewart, M. (1975) *Keynes and After*, London: Penguin.

Storey, D. (1982) *Entrepreneurship and the New Firm*, London: Croom Helm.

Storey, D. (ed.) (1985) *Small Firms and Regional Development*, Cambridge: Cambridge University Press.

Storey, D. and Johnson, S. (1986) 'Job generation in Britain', *International Small Business Journal* 4, 4.

Storey, D., Watson, R. and Wynarczyk, P. (1988) *Fast Growth Small Businesses*, London, Department of Employment Research Paper 67.

Sykes, A. (1967) 'The cohesion of trade union workshop organisation', Sociology, 1, 2.

Timmons, J., Snollen, L. and Dingee, A. (1977) *New Venture Creation*, Homewood: Irwin.

Tomlinson, J. (1982) *The Unequal Struggle*, London: University Paperbacks.

Treadgold, A. (1988) 'Information technology and the independent retail business', *International Small Business Journal* 7, 3: 10–28.

Watkins, D. and Chaplin, P. (1986) 'Development needs in the creation of new co-opeative businesses' in P. Lewis (ed) *Success and Failure in Small Business*, Aldershot: Gower.

Watkins, D., Stanworth, J. and Westrip, A. (eds) (1982) *Stimulating Small Firms*, Aldershot: Gower.

Watson, J. and Watson, D. (1984) 'The female entrepreneur', *International Small Business Journal* 2, 4.

Weber, M. (1978) *Economy and Society*, Berkley: University of California.

Welsh and Young (1984) 'Male and female entrepreneurial characteristics and behaviour', *International Small Business Journal*, 2, 4.

Westrip, A. (1982) 'Effects of employment legislation on small firms', in D. Watkins, J. Stanworth, and A. Westrip (eds) (1982).

Wildsmith, J. (1984) 'Small firms policy – an empty box?', *Journal of Industrial Affairs* 11, 1: 19–26.

Winkler, J. (1977) 'The corporate economy' in R. Scase (ed.) *Industrial Society: Class, Cleavage and Control*, London, George Allen & Unwin.

Wood, S. (1982) *The Degradation of Work*, London: Hutchinson.

Woolham, J. (1988) 'The relationship between aims and objectives in small/medium-sized workers' co-operatives', *International Small Business Journal* 6, 4: 20–32.

Wright, E. O. (1978) *Class, Crisis and the State*, London: Verso.

Wright, E. O. (1985) *Classes*, London: Verso.

Zeitlin, J. (1979) 'Craft, control and the division of labour', *Cambridge Journal of Economics* 3.

Subject Index

Name Index